Express yourself.

Show your true colors.

Let yourself go.

Make It Yours!

MAKE IT YOURS!

Editor: Brian Kramer
Senior Associate Design Director: Ken Carlson
Project Editor and Writer: Jan Soults Walker
Contributing Art Director: Mary Pat Crowley
Contributing Writer: Kellie Kramer
Contributing Photographers: Pam Francis, Scott Little, Janet Mesic Mackie, T. Miyasaki, Jeff Noble, Alise O'Brien, Danny Piassick, William Stites, Rick Taylor, Paul Whicheloe (Anyway Productions Inc.)
Contributing Project Designers: Jilann Severson, Amy Tincher-Durik
Copy Chief: Terri Fredrickson
Copy and Production Editor: Victoria Forlini
Editorial Operations Manager: Karen Schirm
Managers, Book Production: Pam Kvitne, Marjorie J. Schenkelberg, Rick von Holdt
Contributing Copy Editor: Jane Woychick
Contributing Proofreaders: Sue Fetters, Heidi Johnson, Brenda Scott Royce
Editorial and Design Assistants: Kaye Chabot, Karen McFadden, Mary Lee Gavin

Meredith® Books
Editor in Chief: Linda Raglan Cunningham
Design Director: Matt Strelecki
Executive Editor, Home Decorating and Design: Denise L. Caringer

Publisher: James D. Blume
Executive Director, Marketing: Jeffrey Myers
Executive Director, New Business Development: Todd M. Davis
Executive Director, Sales: Ken Zagor
Director, Operations: George A. Susral
Director, Production: Douglas M. Johnston
Business Director: Jim Leonard

Vice President and General Manager: Douglas J. Guendel

Meredith Publishing Group
President, Publishing Group: Stephen M. Lacy
Vice President-Publishing Director: Bob Mate

Meredith Corporation
Chairman and Chief Executive Officer: William T. Kerr

In Memoriam: E. T. Meredith III (1933—2003)

***Trading Spaces* Book Development Team**
Kathy Davidov, Executive Producer, TLC
Roger Marmet, General Manager, TLC
Tom Farrell, Executive Producer, Banyan Productions
Sharon M. Bennett, Senior Vice President, Strategic Partnerships & Licensing
Carol LeBlanc, Vice President, Marketing, Strategic Partnerships
Erica Jacobs Green, Publishing Manager
Elizabeth Bakacs, Creative Director, Strategic Partnerships

Trading Spaces

MAKE IT YOURS!

Meredith® Books
Des Moines, Iowa

Trading
Spaces

contents......

6 Introduction
Peg your perfect decorating scheme by taking the Now You're Stylin' Quiz.

10 Sleek and Modern
Toss out the excess and embrace the stress-free beauty of spaces distinguished by clean lines and no clutter.

24 Très Classique
Bring these timeless looks to your house and you may never have to redecorate again.

48 Why Be Shy?
It's time to come out of hiding and put exciting, one-of-a-kind style in the limelight—where it belongs!

68 Come On Over
Like a porch swing or a terry cloth robe, these room designs are naturally welcoming and warm.

90 A World View
Exotic adventures are only steps away when you lavish a space with details captured from faraway places.

102 Charmed, They're Sure
Every room needs that almost intangible "something special." Glean these spaces for delightful features that are sure to charm.

124 It's Like This...
A swatch of fabric, an heirloom dish, or a striking piece of artwork—these are just a few of the everyday items that could inspire the room of your dreams.

136 So Smile Already!
Begin and end every day on a happy note when you live in spaces spiced with fun and humor. These rooms offer a few laughs you'll love.

158 Episodes Guide   174 Index

Find Your

Adding simple custom touches to basic furniture, fabrics, and accessories gives you a designer look for less—plus you can put your one-of-a-kind stamp on your spaces.

During Designer Chat—the segment near the end of each episode of *Trading Spaces* when Paige and the designers discuss and celebrate room transformations—the designers frequently point out that a space or some piece of furniture already had "good bones." The designers usually go on to say that a few custom touches were all the room or furniture piece needed to become truly special.

Trading Spaces makeovers have the advantage of professional designers, skilled carpenters, and behind-the-scenes helpers (not to mention the television magic of those sped-up video segments!), but that doesn't mean you can't make your own real-world transformations. Fresh style and good design don't come from a particular store, catalog, or website. Great style comes from taking solid, basic items and making them yours with paint treatments, distinctive trims, special fabrics, and personalized accessories.

Of course you want your home to look good and function well for you, your family, and your friends. But more important, you want to feel like the space is yours. You want others to look at your redecorating projects and say that the new look is totally you.

That's where the *Trading Spaces* difference comes into play. The success of any makeover—for the *Trading Spaces* designers and for you—is in the details. These details are the dozens of little ways you express yourself in your spaces.

Many decorating and design television shows and books tell you to follow specific instructions to get a cookie-cutter "appropriate" look. Not so with *Trading Spaces* or this book. Instead, the focus is on *you.* (Nice for a change, huh?) This book helps you figure out what styles you like, what you love about

6

Style!

your home, and what you'd like to change. It also provides easy techniques and simple projects to help you create beautiful rooms and furnishings that are *100-percent you*.

✳ Detailed tours of nearly two dozen *Trading Spaces* rooms offer loads of information and ideas to jump-start your room transformations.

✳ How-to techniques teach you the skills you need to redo an entire room—or a single piece of furniture.

✳ *Trading Spaces* Toolbox sidebars introduce you to the tools you'll need to make your decorating dreams reality.

✳ 16 Make It Yours projects show you how to get gorgeous custom looks from basic store-bought items such as mirrors, lamps, pillows, and side tables.

If you rent, don't worry—you don't have to own your home to make it yours. This book offers dozens of simple ideas for creating fabulous custom looks that still allow you to reclaim your damage deposit. You've got ideas. You've got passions. Now—in your hands, in this book—you've got the resources to begin expressing them. Turn the page and get ready to make your home truly yours!

TOOLBOX

Custom Tricks of the Trade

Customize just about anything with these easy decorating tools and supplies.

The *Trading Spaces* crew knows how to make even the blandest store-bought bookshelf a beautiful custom creation. Fortunately, makeovers rarely require hours of work, lots of money, or advanced design skills. A successful transformation often comes down to adding the right custom touches at the right time.

Be prepared to take on projects large and small; outfit your decorating supply kit with these *Trading Spaces* favorites:

✳ **Paint pens.** Embellish wood, fabric, window treatments, and more, quickly and boldly.

✳ **Tissue paper.** Decoupage layers of color onto a variety of surfaces.

✳ **Spray adhesive.** Apply to paper, fabric, light woods, or plastic sheeting for an instant bond.

✳ **Fusible iron-on tape.** Use instead of a sewing machine to hem curtains, tabletop accessories, slipcovers, pillows, and fabric panels.

✳ **Seed beads**. String them for rich cordlike trim or glue them to flat surfaces for shimmering texture.

✳ **Masking tape.** Mark off stripes, plaids, and other graphic shapes prior to painting.

✳ **Disposable sponge brushes.** Use to apply a coat of paint, glue, or stain—and then simply discard.

✳ **Tea lights**. Add an instant touch of warmth to tabletops, floral arrangements, display shelves, and more.

Now You're Stylin' Quiz

Whether you're a seasoned decorating pro with a look all your own or you're only beginning to figure out your style (and perhaps yourself), take the following 17-question quiz to help identify the stuff you like, avoid the things you don't like, and begin to create and express your signature style in every room of your home.

1. My personal theme song should be
a. Beethoven's "Ode to Joy"
b. "Wild Thing"
c. "(Sittin' on) The Dock of the Bay"
d. "Cheek to Cheek"
e. "What the World Needs Now Is Love"

2. My idea of the perfect place to nap is
a. A cherry four-poster bed, snuggled up in a fluffy down comforter
b. A hammock in the shade, with light breezes blowing
c. The couch, under a favorite quilt
d. A lacquered platform bed, covered in red satin sheets
e. A wicker daybed, underneath yards of gauze and netting

3. If I could choose one *Trading Spaces* cast member to go shopping with, I'd most like to shop
a. Department stores with Laurie
b. An open-air market with Doug
c. A flea market with Frank
d. The hottest New York boutiques with Hildi
e. A quaint seaside town with Gen

4. My favorite movie duo is
a. Humphrey Bogart and Ingrid Bergman
b. John Travolta and Olivia Newton-John
c. Katharine Hepburn and Spencer Tracy
d. Fred Astaire and Ginger Rogers
e. Ryan O'Neal and Ali MacGraw

5. The one *Trading Spaces* cast member I'd invite to my birthday party is
a. Laurie
b. Kia
c. Frank
d. Vern
e. Gen

6. My ideal space for hosting a party with friends would be
a. A dining room with lush centerpieces and exquisite linens
b. A beach cabana with retro-tiki attitude
c. A living room with piles of pillows and afghans
d. A private table reserved at a French bistro
e. A gazebo at night, decorated with strings of paper lanterns

7. If I were attending the Oscars, I'd wear
a. A ball gown with crinoline
b. A magenta sari
c. A simple pantsuit
d. A silver lamé halter dress
e. A gauzy frock with beaded trim

8. If I could live inside the world of a movie, I'd choose
a. Howards End
b. Moulin Rouge
c. It's a Wonderful Life
d. Breakfast at Tiffany's
e. Out of Africa

9. I'd describe my dream car as
a. A navy blue Cadillac
b. A lime green VW Beetle
c. A Ford Explorer with comfy seats
d. A silver Lexus sedan with all the options
e. A red Mustang convertible

10. I love the feel of
a. Leather upholstery
b. Woven rattan
c. Warm suede
d. Marble tile
e. Soft chenille

11. I love the smell of
a. Vanilla and cinnamon
b. Curry and jasmine
c. Chocolate chip cookies, hot from the oven
d. Roses
e. Lavender and orange blossoms

12. I adore the taste of

a. A perfectly grilled steak

b. Thai peanut chicken

c. Barbecued ribs

d. Champagne and strawberries

e. Tea and petit fours

c. Have a cookout

d. Sit at the snack bar and wish I were elsewhere

e. Read a good book

13. If I could only have one pair of shoes (!), I'd choose

a. Black high heels or oxfords

b. Chunky sneakers

c. Comfortable sandals

d. Strappy stilettos or patent leather lace-ups

e. Suede clogs

15. At antiques stores, I find myself drawn to

a. Finely crafted wood tables, dressers, and picture frames

b. Soda fountain signs

c. Toys and board games from the 1950s

d. Vintage jewelry

e. Postcards and old photos

14. When I visit the beach, I typically

a. Play in the waves and surf

b. Search for shells

16. My friends jokingly say that I must have been separated at birth from

a. Laurie

b. Kia

c. Frank

d. Vern

e. Gen

17. My dream date includes

a. Dinner and dancing

b. Snowboarding and sushi

c. Burgers and good friends

d. Cigars and cognac

e. Moonlight and jasmine

To score this amazingly scientific quiz:

Tally the number of times you answered a, b, c, d, or e. The letter you chose most frequently indicates your general decorating, design, and color attitudes, as listed in the chart below.

If you answered: This is your attitude:

a. Classic	You know a good thing when you see it! You gravitate toward traditional styles (with a few twists, of course). You want to furnish your home with looks and colors that can last a lifetime, adding new accessories and decorative touches along the way. Look for regal, luxurious colors.
b. Funky	As in other areas of your life, you'll try anything in your home decor. You look for unusual materials and exotic influences. Color is fun and feisty for you—with lots of contrasts.
c. Casual	For you, comfort is paramount. You want to look good, but not by sacrificing any comfort. Warm, easy color that envelopes your soul and no-fuss neutrals are just what the color doctor ordered.
d. Chic	You've got style and you like to show it, whether spare and minimal or sleek and stunning. Color should be neutral and subtly blended, with bold, showstopping accents that "pop" when you look at a room.
e. Romantic	You want your home to take you away from the hustle and pressures of life. You strive to add personal, intimate touches to your home and furniture. Your colors are soft, soothing, and relaxing.

If your answers are spread out between several options, you may have an eclectic style, built around mixing and matching the looks and items you love. Who knows? You may be on your way to creating an entirely new style for the 21st century.

SLEEK AND MODERN

10

Chapter I: Sleek and Modern Clean lines—whether they're in architecture, fashion, or even an automobile—instantly capture your attention. If you're ready to toss out the clutter and live in a low-stress environment, let these unfettered beauties set your imagination in motion.

An electric nailer definitely simplified the process of sheathing these bedroom walls in maple—although it was still a time-consuming project. To learn more about electric nailers, turn to page 116.

Now and Zen Warm Up

STYLE LESSON: Wood unifies and warms.
BACKGROUND: A high ceiling offers drama in this bedroom but makes the space seem cold. Vern tackles this common design dilemma by wrapping the walls and the ceiling with sleek wood panels for a restful, uncluttered look that exudes warmth.

Warming Trend ◄

Clear furniture-grade maple sheets serve as Vern's savvy solution for making this voluminous, vaulted master bedroom more intimate and sophisticated. The short end walls are lavishly dressed in deep purple paint and fabric; the maple lends a layer of elegance to long sidewalls and the peaked ceiling. The 25 sheets cost Vern a mere $10 each— "unheard of," Vern says, less than one-third of the typical price. Leftover sheets, cut into 5-inch-wide strips, form a battenlike grid pattern over whole sheets, which are affixed to wall studs with a nail gun. The result is a clean, modern version of a cozy paneled library look. Rather than darken the room with stain, Vern finished the panels with clear polyurethane sealer, letting the light wood introduce its natural golden glow to the room. The platform bed and end tables, which are custom-built from naturally finished birch plywood, retain the simple lines and lighter appearance of the maple wood walls. Bedding and pillows in an array of purples pull the palette into the heart of the room.

Lofty Ideals ◄

Rather than stop the wood panels at the top of the walls, Vern covered the vaulted ceiling—a job that kept Vern and the neighbors up all night. A trio of contemporary light fixtures, suspended from cables, offers a sophisticated finish overhead.

Horizontal Vision ▲

Reflecting the long, low lines of the platform bed, this birch plywood shelving unit spans outward rather than upward. It's specially designed to hold the television, VCR, and DVD player and offers enough space for books, photograph display, and collections. The clear polyurethane finish keeps the look compatible with the maple walls.

Plywood Versus MDF
Get the lowdown on sheet goods for your projects.

You'll often see the *Trading Spaces* designers requesting projects built from either plywood or medium-density fiberboard (MDF). So what's the difference? Plywood is made up of veneer layers; it's very strong because the grain in each layer runs perpendicular to the grain of adjacent layers. For a smooth, attractive outside layer, choose A-rated plywood. Birch plywood is popular because its grain is light and the surface looks good painted or stained. Oak or birch plywood costs $30–$35 for a ½-inch-thick 4×8-foot sheet.

Medium-density fiberboard is made up of wood particles that are bonded with resin and compressed. The material is hard and can be cut and used like plywood, but it isn't as strong as plywood. Still, you'll pay less for MDF—about $15 for a ½-inch-thick 4×8-foot sheet. MDF looks good painted; or you can purchase MDF covered with melamine—a durable plastic surface that comes in colors.

Because the edges of plywood and MDF aren't pretty, you'll need to finish exposed edges with veneer or moldings or with 1× lumber cut to fit.

Reflecting on Details ◀

Special details don't have to be expensive or expansive. Vern found eight diminutive mirrored sconces for about $7 each. The sconces each hold a taper candle, "so you see a reflection of the flicker in the mirror." When hanging multiple items in a row on a wall, use an extra-long carpenter's level to ensure a straight, level lineup.

For visual impact without clutter, repeat a single material throughout a room or display multiples of one type of item.

Cutting Plywood

With any woodworking project, measure twice, cut once.

Cutting those big sheets of plywood is easier than you think when you team the right tools with a few smart strategies. Choose a circular saw or table saw for fast, safe cuts.

1 To cut a large sheet of plywood by yourself, equip a **circular saw** with a plywood-cutting blade. Support the plywood sheet on 2×4s laid on the floor and cut as shown (A).

2 To rip plywood (cut with the grain) with an assistant, unplug the saw and adjust the fence to the necessary width. Plug in the saw and have a helper assist as you position the sheet against the fence (B). Be careful not to apply too much pressure to the fence or you could knock it out of position. Turn on the saw; then feed the sheet through the saw, supporting the sheet as it moves (C).

3 To crosscut plywood (cut across the grain) on a **table saw** without assistance, remove the rip fence and lock the miter gauge at zero. (If you're unsure which features are the rip fence and miter gauge, refer to the owner's manual.) Reverse the miter gauge in the groove and position the plywood sheet firmly against it (D) Align the cutting mark with the blade and start the saw. Halfway through the sheet, stop the saw. Back the miter gauge out of the groove and slip the gauge into the front of the groove as shown (E). Finish making the cut.

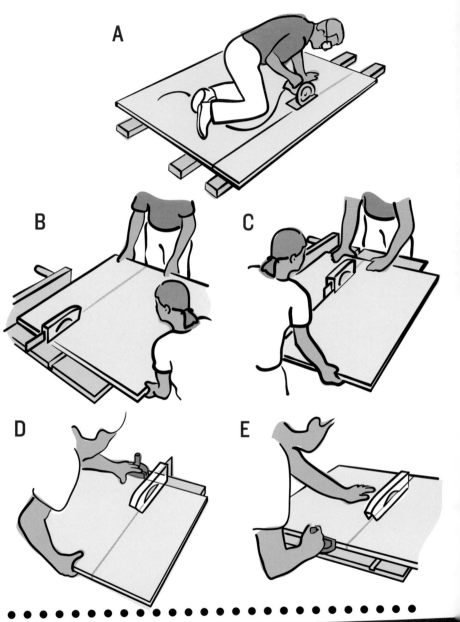

Table Saws

Prized for power and precision, table saws can save time.

If you love do-it-yourself projects, you're bound to get a lot of use from a table saw, so choose carefully. Look for a table saw that's solid so that it doesn't vibrate as you cut. In most cases, you'll be glad you spent the extra money on a freestanding table saw rather than buying a bench-top model. Buy the most powerful belt-driven model you can afford. Examine the rip fence and check that it clamps firmly in place parallel to the blade. Test the rip fence to see if it moves easily; the crosscutting guide should easily slide in the groove too. For durability and splinter-free cuts, invest in a carbide-tip 10-inch combination blade.

Make It Yours: Pillows

Plush, plump, poofy—any way you squeeze 'em, purchased pillows can be personalized with simple embellishments. Here are stylin' ideas for perking up pillows.

Button, Button

Assorted buttons give this pillow three-dimensional appeal. You'll find selections of buttons at fabric and crafts stores. If you prefer the look of vintage buttons, check flea markets, thrift stores, garage sales, and antiques shops. Also, look around your own home; clothing that's ready for the rag bag may have some great buttons. After you gather buttons, draw the dimensions of the pillow top on paper and mark which section you want to cover with buttons. Lay out vintage or reproduction buttons in the desired pattern. Sew the buttons to the pillow top using your design idea as a guide. Use quality fabric glue to secure decorative multiple bands of satin cording around the outer edge of the pillow.

Zip It Up

Dress up a pillow with this zippy striped design. Purchase enough zippers to cover the entire pillow top, varying the kind, color, and length of zippers. You can also remove and use zippers from old clothing; check thrift stores for bargains. For variety, consider substituting two short zippers for one long zipper if you wish. If a zipper is too long, trim the ends with pinking shears to fit the pillow face. Lay out the desired stripe pattern on a table, alternating the direction of the zippers for interest. Avoid placing two rows of short zippers next to each other. Glue the zippers to the pillow top with quality fabric glue. If you want to be able to operate the zippers, keep the glue toward the outer edges.

Just Your Type

Let your pillow make a soft-spoken statement with this subtle slipcover. Print out text using an inkjet or laser printer. Or use a photocopier to enlarge and copy pages of text from a copyright-free book. Tape pages together to assemble enough words to cover an area slightly larger than the pillow top.

For easy tracing, tape the pages of text to a sunny window. Then tape lightweight semisheer fabric over the pages and trace lettering with a permanent fabric marker. Cut out two pieces of the sheer fabric for a slipcover, adding ½ inch for seam allowances. Stitch a hem, sewing in ribbon ties on one edge of each piece. With right sides facing, stitch together three sides of the slipcover. Turn right side out, slip the cover over a pillow, and tie to secure. For a bit of colorful fun, stitch or glue silk flowers at each tie.

Two-Sided Masterpiece

This pillow displays different artwork. You need an ink-jet shirt transfer kit and access to a computer and an ink-jet printer. Copy or scan artwork from a copyright-free book (or draw your own designs) onto transfer paper. Flip the image—especially if it includes letters or numbers. Cut two pieces of muslin to fit the pillow front and back, adding 1 inch for a hem. Press under edges; secure hems with iron-on tape. Iron the transfers onto the muslin, following kit directions. Use grommet pliers to add grommets along the edges of the muslin pieces. Sandwich a pillow between muslin pieces and thread two lengths of ribbon through the grommets, front to back, to secure both pieces around the pillow.

L'INSTANT
TAITTINGER

Before

A cookie-cutter builder's-grade fireplace
and lots of white and beige make this
living room lackluster. The homeowners
hope for a special treatment that will
distinguish their fireplace from others in
neighboring homes.

Champagne Elegance *Can a bit of the bubbly beautify your abode?*

STYLE LESSON: Clean-lined artwork prompts chic style.
BACKGROUND: Gen dresses up a plain fireplace in a sleek black wood facade as sophisticated and stylish as the dress of a diva in a French poster. In the end, it's difficult to say which is more elegant: the room or Gen attired in a strapless black gown.

Poster Child ◀

Inspired by the graceful image and rich colors of a French champagne poster, Gen sets plain family room walls aglow with a sunny tricolor paint wash (a yellow base coat topped with yellow- and orange-tinted glazes). Black accents add elegance, especially to the new fluted wood fireplace facade constructed by Ty.

Art for a Song ◀

Great-looking artwork doesn't have to break your budget. Here, a poster and a pair of wine advertisements offer inexpensive visual punch. Narrow black frames unify the grouping and repeat the black accents used throughout the room. Adding lamps with black shades atop the black-painted table emphasizes the sophisticated use of black as an accent.

Fan Flair ▼

Ceiling fans may not be a favorite among the *Trading Spaces* designers, but they are a practical feature that can be dressed up. Gen added a molded ceiling medallion and applied silver rub to this fan to give it some style. Medallions such as these are often fabricated from plastic that can be painted to stand out from or blend with the color of the ceiling.

Vavoom Fabrics ▲

Setting an elegant, solid-color stage of washed gold walls, velvety black pillows, and a splashy red rug allowed Gen to customize the furniture with unexpected pattern. Bold black peonies on a white background transform ordinary sofas into graphically gorgeous centerpieces. Gen and a neighbor laid the fabric facedown on each sofa and pinned and cut the pieces to fit. *For more about making slipcovers, see page 36.*

Cable Hook-ups ▲
Gen lends new meaning to the term "cable TV" with this idea: Two lengths of cable hold a simply made wood TV shelf. The cable adds a linear element to the room without drawing attention away from the fireplace.

Glowing Reviews ▲
The color-wash wall treatment isn't the only thing glowing in this living room. A pair of candle sconces with clear glass tulip-shape shades offers a pretty detail on the walls.

> " By balancing the enormity of the fireplace with this big TV on the other side," Gen says, "it makes the TV feel like it's not taking up the whole room. "

More Cable Creations

Use stainless-steel cable for fashion and function.

Visit any home center and you'll likely find a section offering stainless-steel cable in various diameters. Cut the cable with bolt cutters, loop the cable through an eyehook, then clamp the loop closed with a fastener called a ferrule. Other nifty hardware, such as turnbuckles, can add style and strength to the cable assembly. Here are a few ideas for using stainless-steel cable at home.

* Fashion a railing with lengths of cable stretched between two walls or a pair of posts.
* Install a framework of steel cable above a bed and drape it with fabric to create a canopy.
* Use cable to hang a chandelier.
* Drill holes in the corners of a series of shelves. Thread the cable through the holes, crimp ferrules onto the cable beneath each shelf, and suspend the shelves from the ceiling.

Steel Cable Style

Wherever you place them, these steel cable projects may steal the show.

Steel cable isn't only for rooms with industrial or strictly contemporary styles. These projects allow you to use steel cable in nearly any setting.

Gallery Chic

To hang a framed piece of artwork using steel cable (A), twist two screw eyes into the top corners of the picture frame. Thread a length of cable through one screw eye, form a loop, and secure the loop with a ferrule. This metal sleeve can be crimped with a special tool; or use a vise grip and some muscle to clamp the ferrule around the loop end. Pass the end of the cable through a pulley (B) and through the other screw eye. Form a loop and clip off the excess with a cable cutter; then clamp the loop end with a ferrule. Hang the pulley from an S hook and hang the S hook from a screw eye (B) that's secured to a ceiling joist or anchored with a hollow-wall fastener. *See page 54 for information on hollow-wall anchors.*

Clip-On Curtains

Hanging curtain panels—or even a vintage tablecloth—is a snap when you use this approach. Drive a screw hook at each side of a window (C). Cut cable long enough to fit between the hooks, allowing excess to form a loop at each end. Clamp each loop with a ferrule. Equally space clip-on rings across the top of a piece of fabric or curtain panel (D) and thread the rings onto the cable. Suspend the cable between the two screw hooks.

A — S hook, Pulley, Steel cable, Ferrule, Screw eye

B — S hook, Pulley, Steel cable

C

D — Clip-on ring

TOOLBOX

Wire Cutters

With this handy tool, it's OK to be snippy.

You've watched enough episodes of *Trading Spaces* to know that a wire cutter is an essential tool—especially if you plan to get rid of the ceiling fan and install a new fixture! For wiring projects, look for combination wire cutters-stripping tools, which are designed to cut through wire and strip off insulation. A wire cutter-stripper with a narrow nose allows you to reach into tight places. Wire gauge markings should be easy to read on both sides of the nose for stripping wire from either direction. Wire cutters work for smaller jobs too, such as clipping the wire stems on silk flowers. Look for lightweight wire cutters to reduce fatigue. If you decide to experiment with any steel cable projects, purchase a bolt or cable cutter to easily snip through the cable. *See page 142 for details on installing a ceiling fixture.*

Media Center Solutions

Strapped for ideas on what to do with your television and stereo? Look for storage options that complement your decor and keep electronic components accessible.

Flip it. Think of ready-to-assemble shelf units as building blocks you can turn any way you desire. Flip, flop, rotate, and adjust the shelves in these units until the shape and space satisfy your needs. Gen dismantled a vertical entertainment center and reassembled the pieces to make a custom stereo and TV unit in Alexandria: Riefton Court.

Spread it. Rather than clumping all your equipment in one dark, dull group, consider spacing out the pieces on a large shelf, an entire wall, or even multiple walls. In an Albuquerque living room, Hildi hung various boxes in a flowing arrangement on a wall and fit one piece of audiovisual equipment into each box.

Hide it. If stereo equipment doesn't mesh with the decor of your space, conceal the pieces behind metal screens, curtains, doors, or wood panels. In California: Grenadine Way, Frank covered two cubbyholes above a mantel with hinged doors that he painted with decorative tribal stripes.

Hang it. When floor and wall space are at a premium in small or multipurpose rooms, look up to the ceiling for audiovisual storage solutions. In Portland, Doug placed the television for a home theater on a large wooden platform suspended by cables from the ceiling.

23

Paint it. Fitting a big-screen TV into a decor is a huge challenge. Rather than build or purchase cabinetry for large-scale electronics, use paint to connect the equipment with the scheme. Gen helped a big-screen TV fit into a living room by painting a block of light color on the wall behind the TV.

Chapter 2: Très Classique Isn't it nice to know that some things, like long-stemmed roses for instance, never go out of style? Each of these rooms offers timelessness—they'll seem beautiful tomorrow, next week, next year, and perhaps even years from now.

TRÈS

CLASSIQUE

Before

TCR 01:39.57:23
V---- A----

More than a decade old, the wall border is about to get the boot; but that's OK—the homeowners say they have fallen out of love with their own decorating and are ready for bright and colorful.

Toile Terrific

Hildi uses French fabric to transform walls from ordinary to "Ooh la la!"

STYLE LESSON: For classic looks, choose fabrics with timeless appeal.
BACKGROUND: Hildi bagged this beautiful red, white, and black toile fabric in Paris, but toile is a hot item in the United States too and available in many patterns and color combinations. Use it all over as Hildi does or sprinkle it around for some splashy French effects.

Lavish Fabric on a Favorite Room ◀

When you're ready for a classic yet dramatic change, a sure strategy is to envelop a room in the spectacular patterns of toile. In this case, black-and-white Oriental-theme scenes grace a red background, offering a feast for the eyes and an atmosphere that's both cozy and elegant. Designers love to use this picturesque material in quantity; Hildi lavishes it on the walls, then disperses it in window treatments and a duvet. To balance the abundance of rich red color, solid-charcoal pillows line up at the head of the bed; at the foot of the bed, the sofa wears an off-white cotton slipcover. Drawn to the curving corners of this $25 thrift store find, Hildi updates the piece by trading three seat cushions for one long one and eliminating the back cushion (because she prefers a sofa that sits deep). "I can see the beauty in many things," Hildi says, "and the curves on the sofa have

Oriental flair." At $5 each, the lamps are also thrift store bargains. Paint and new shades give each one a fresh start. *To learn a method for hanging fabric, turn to page 30. For tips on making slipcovers, turn to page 36.*

Shadow Boxing ▼

Hildi fired up the saw to make these chic shadow boxes herself, using MDF for the frames and backs. In each box, an Oriental figurine rests on a black-painted block of wood that's screwed to the back. For a soft, textural finish inside each frame, the backboard is covered in off-white canvas cut from a drop cloth. Set against the red toile wall, the simple black frames stand out vividly. *The shadow boxes require only basic cube construction—a technique you can master by following the steps on page 148. For tips on cutting plywood and MDF, see page 16.*

Using double-wide fabric, Hildi worked with the neighbors to staple swaths to the wall. When using fabric with an allover pattern, purchase extra fabric so that you can match the pattern at all the seams.

27

Ceiling Subtlety ▲

Charcoal-color paint makes the ceiling almost disappear in the room. This fixture offers unobtrusive lighting. Its simple styling allows the fabric walls to stand out as the star of the room.

Birds of a Feather ▶

Vases can hold more than flowers. In this vignette, pheasant feathers stand tall and stylishly in clear glass vases. The feathers and a framed print of a robin pick up on the bird motif in the toile.

Glue Gun

Holster one of these in your home tool kit for a quick stick between surfaces.

Stand in the glue gun section of any crafts store and you might be surprised by the assortment. Glue guns and glue sticks come in regular and miniature sizes and in hot-melt and low-temperature varieties.

Hot-melt guns heat up to more than 350°F and offer a secure bond between surfaces that can stand up to the high temperature, such as wood.

Low-temperature glue guns heat up to 200°F—cooler than hot-melt guns and easier on your fingers—and are an ideal choice for joining materials that could melt or burn when exposed to high temperatures, such as foam and paper.

Some glue guns can operate at either high or low temperatures. Choose the appropriate type of glue stick for the job. Some glue guns come with a variety of nozzle tips that release glue in wide or thin streams or ribbons.

Most glue guns are easy to use: Plug it in, let it heat up, and point the nozzle where you want the glue to flow. Pull the trigger to release the glue.

Watch your fingers when using a hot-melt gun because the hot glue hurts when it lands on bare skin. Consider wearing fabric or leather gloves to protect your hands when working with hot glue. Also, equip your work area with a heatproof surface or a glue gun rest so you have a safe place to set the glue gun when you take a break.

28

Armoire Amour ▲

Designed to complement the graceful lines of the sofa, this custom-built armoire features an undulating design with doors that arc outward, concave open shelves, and towel bars that stand in as handles. The rich faux-painted finish—red paint toned down with brown that was rubbed on and off—creates the illusion that this might be a vintage Oriental piece.

Dress Up Walls with Fabric

Starch lets you stick and peel fabric with ease.

Covering walls with fabric is a great way to achieve a custom look; it's also a clever cover-up for cracks, dents, and other flaws. Rather than attach fabric with a staple gun, stick the fabric on with laundry starch. When you're tired of the look, simply peel the fabric off the wall, throw it in the washing machine, and use it again for another project. It's an especially smart decorating tool for renters. Here are two easy ways to make fabric stick:

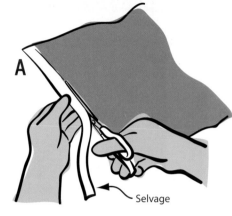

B C

Selvage

D

Soak and Stick

1 **Clean the wall surface** to remove dirt and grease. Cover high-gloss paint with a wallpaper primer.

2 **Purchase liquid starch** and enough 100-percent-cotton fabric to cover the walls. Measure the height of the walls and add a few inches to the dimension to allow for a temporary overlap. Cut off selvage and cut panel to desired length (A).

3 **Soak panel in a large container** filled with several inches of undiluted liquid starch (B). Fold fabric and squeeze out excess starch (C). (To avoid stretching the fabric, don't wring or twist.)

4 **Start in an inconspicuous corner** and smooth fabric onto the wall with your hands (D); allow an inch or so of fabric to overlap at the top and bottom of the wall. Also let fabric overlap onto window or door moldings. Don't trim excess yet.

5 **Cut subsequent fabric panels,** matching the pattern before cutting. Repeat steps 3 and 4 until walls are covered. (You don't have to cover the entire wall; you may want to apply fabric above or below a chair rail or in vertical accent strips.) Let fabric dry. Use a sharp utility knife to trim excess.

Roll and Stick

1 **After following steps 1 and 2** of "Soak and Stick" directions, pour undiluted liquid starch into a paint pan and use a foam roller or sponge to apply starch to the top half of the wall; roll or sponge starch only as far as the width of the panel.

2 **Press fabric panel in place** with your hands (D), allowing an inch or so to overlap onto the ceiling or crown molding. If necessary, use pushpins or tacks at the top to prevent the panel from slipping.

3 **Roll starch onto the bottom portion of the wall** beneath the fabric panel and finish pressing into place with your hands. Allow at least 1 inch of fabric to overlap onto the baseboard. To smooth and secure the fabric panel to the wall, roll, brush, or sponge additional starch onto the top side of the panel, smoothing the surface as you go. Remove pins or tacks holding the panel in place and move on to the next panel, repeating the steps to complete the room. Allow panels to overlap onto window and door casings about 1 inch. Match the pattern before cutting the panel to length. Let panels dry; then use a sharp utility knife to cut fabric that overlaps the window and door casings. crown molding, or baseboards.

Custom Furniture

You don't have to make do with pieces that don't work for you.

When you make a piece of furniture for yourself, you can shape the look to suit your room and your needs. No one else will have anything like it!

Think of seating as building blocks. Look for or build upholstered seating pieces in a variety of sizes and styles for maximum flexibility. In a basement rec room in Quakertown: Quakers Way, Hildi built a nine-piece sectional with three chairs and six ottomans that could be arranged in dozens of configurations, depending on the homeowners' needs.

Combine function in one piece. Make your seating play multiple roles by building reclining elements, tabletops, storage compartments, and more. In Gen's Santa Fe living room, Ty built a platform couch that includes two wooden frames that flank the upholstered middle portion. Rope woven horizontally across the frames forms rustic end tables.

Update a classic. Take a favorite style of seating—wing chairs, Chippendale dining chairs, or other popular looks—and spice it up with new fabrics, embellishments, finishes, or shapes. In a Washington, D.C., basement TV room, Doug improved on a classic beanbag chair by sewing a wall-length beanbag sofa that he filled with plastic-foam packing peanuts.

Go for mobility. For entertaining or hanging out, choose seating that easily moves and adapts to changing needs. Look for lightweight cushions and pillows, legs on casters, and adjustable seat heights. Hildi's custom "pillow pods" offer versatile, casual seating in a New Jersey bedroom.

Build to suit. What do you get when you combine a basic wood cube, a foam cushion, and fabric? Fantastic custom seating, of course! In a Colorado living room, Doug built a couch by covering 6-inch-thick foam pieces with fabric and resting them on wood rectangles laid out in an L shape.

31

Double-Duty Decor

STYLE LESSON: Two classic styles equal one lasting look.
BACKGROUND: Edward appreciates the way that Greek Revival and Oriental styles can merge so effortlessly. He blends the elements beautifully in this bedroom and cleverly disguises the headboard to serve as an architectural feature and a floor plan fix.

● ●

Dynamic Duos ◀

Edward decided to divide one bedroom into two functional spaces—for sleeping and dressing—and decorate with two timeless styles, Greek and Asian. First he pulled the bed to the center of the room and gave the headboard and footboard a new, soft look with slipcovers. A white-painted mantelpiece, fashioned from moldings and 1× lumber, tops the headboard to create a more substantial divider. One side of the room serves as the sleeping area; the opposite side of the headboard, which faces the closet door, acts as a wall for the bureau.

For the sleeping area, Edward made two plaques—one displays a figurine and another a vase—as expressions of the Greek and Oriental influences that inspired the room.

Soft Touches ▼

Above all else, a bedroom must offer comfort. Introducing generous amounts of fabric is one sure way to achieve that goal. Edward makes the bed more inviting, for example, by wrapping layers of batting around the headboard and footboard before adding slipcovers; the pillows and long silvery bolster add beauty and make the bed irresistible. Rich brown, buttercream, and taupe bedding and slipcovers along with the sienna brown walls and platinum tray ceiling create an air of classic elegance. Beside the bed, one wall features layers of generously gathered fabric panels. The panels serve as a backdrop for artwork; low-voltage puck lights on the soffit lend a subtle glow.

Before

The homeowners of this master bedroom say it's boring and the white has to go. They would like to see all the furniture repositioned to make the space more functional.

33

Gracious Appointments ▲

Salvage yards can be treasure troves of elegant goodies—sometimes at great prices. That's where Edward found this brass chandelier. He began transforming it by removing the glass panes and spray-painting the metal frame black. Black and gold paint markers dress up the panes themselves. Before hanging the light, Edward added a faux-plaster medallion to the ceiling for another classic architectural element. Medallions of this kind are practical too: Sometimes when you change fixtures, you'll discover that the hole in the ceiling is larger than the base of the new fixture. A medallion hides the difference.

The medallion isn't the only fool-the-eye feature: Edward gives the room symmetry by creating a faux window from the fabric and roll-up blinds that dress other windows. Can you tell which window isn't real?

Off-the-Cuff Creations ◄

Beauty beats the budget thanks to a little recycling ingenuity. These oh-so-elegant curtain rods are really cardboard tubes sheathed in fabric; the finials are fabric-covered foam balls glued to the ends of the cardboard tubes.

The cabinet box, which Amy Wynn built with stylish Oriental overtones, stands on legs borrowed from an old flea market vanity. The panel insets in the cabinet doors are woven place mats.

Before you re-cover furniture, improve the shape: Pad dips, flat seats, or skinny arms with layers of batting. If the batting doesn't cling to the piece on its own, baste to keep the batting from slipping.

Room Arranging Kit   Plan before lifting heavy furniture.

If you've ever lugged a bulky sofa from one end of the room to another, only to decide it looked better in the first spot, you'll appreciate this handy decorating tool. Room arranging kits are available in bookstores, home centers, and online and cost as little as $5–$20. Most kits include a guide booklet, graph paper, and furniture templates that allow you to plan and reconfigure a room layout. Make sure that the kit you're buying features the templates you need. Some kits include furniture for the living room, family room, dining room, bedroom, and home office. Other kits are specially designed to plan the layout of a kitchen or bathroom.

Simple Slipcovers

Learn the secrets for creating your own fabric cover-ups.

If you know how to use scissors, pins, and a sewing machine, consider making some custom slipcovers. Follow these basics for beautiful results:

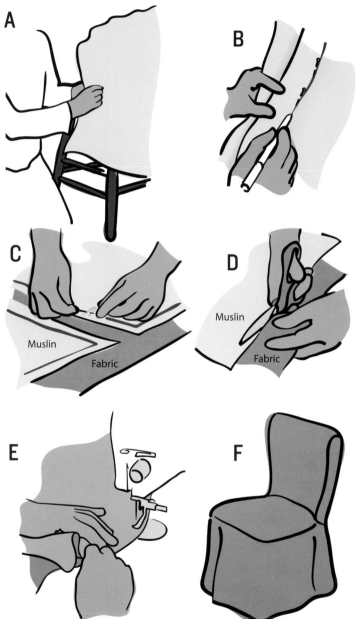

Choose Your Slipcover Strategy:

1 **Fit and pin decorator fabric to the furniture** (A). This is a good approach if you're a novice using inexpensive fabric. If you're a confident sewer, you can use this approach with more expensive fabrics.

2 **Make a muslin pattern first if you are a novice** and plan to use expensive fabric, or if you are experienced but plan to slipcover a chair or sofa with challenging curves. The muslin pattern lets you double-check the fit without wasting fabric.

Fit and Pin

Take rough measurements and estimate yardage. For a tailored skirt (F) measure from the seat of the chair to the floor; then double the fabric to give the skirt weight.

Approach the piece section by section. Lay fabric with the right side facing down over the furniture back, making sure the fabric pattern (if there is one) is straight and centered. Pin the fabric (A) and mark along the pin lines with a fabric marker (B). Remove the fabric from the furniture, take out the pins, and draw a second line ½ inch outside all the marked lines. Cut the fabric, staying slightly outside the second line to allow for error and adjustments, if this is your first slipcover. Skip to "To the Finish."

Make a Muslin Pattern

Follow the instructions under "Fit and Pin," but when you cut the fabric, cut along the outside line rather than allowing so much for adjustments.

Lay the decorator fabric right side up and iron out wrinkles. Pin the muslin pieces to the decorator fabric with the marked side of the muslin up (C). Note how the pattern on the decorator fabric lands within each muslin piece. Cut out the pieces (D).

To the Finish

36 Right sides together, align raw edges of two adjacent pieces and sew (E) using the ½-inch seam allowance. Test-fit every seam and make adjustments before adding the next piece.

Turn the cover right side out and slip over the furniture. Mark where the hem should fall at several places along the bottom edge and remove the slipcover. (Or mark where you need to cut off the excess if you plan to staple the bottom edge of the slipcover to the underside of the piece.) Turn the slipcover wrong side out. Press and hem. Press seams open and trim off any excess. Turn right side out and slip the cover over the furniture. Staple to the underside of the piece if you wish.

Smart Room Arrangements

Decorating a room involves more than paint, fabric, and furnishings: It means thinking about how all the pieces fit into the floor plan.

Focus your furnishings. Dedicate a room to a specific activity such as TV watching, reading, or exercising. Remove any furniture that isn't necessary and arrange remaining pieces for optimal enjoyment of the activity. Gen simplified a narrow Key West living room by removing excess furniture and building a custom L-shape couch with built-in end table arms.

Use furniture rather than walls. Purchase premade unfinished shelving units available at home centers in various heights and widths. Install with a few bolts in the ceiling and floor; then finish the shelves with paint, fabric, or wallcovering. Edward used three shelving units placed side by side to divide a bedroom and provide additional closet space.

Divide a space with furniture. Divide a room by centrally locating large furniture—bookcases, sofas, console tables, and islands. In a Maryland bedroom, Doug placed the bed in the center of the room and added a huge headboard with storage cubes and a desk area on the opposite side.

Divide a space with fabric. If you don't have large furniture for dividing a room, hang fabric from ceiling to floor. In Austin: La Costa Drive, Vern moved the bed to the center of a bonus room and hung a swath of iridescent fabric behind the headboard to curtain off a desk and sewing area.

Connect a space with details. For large multipurpose spaces, cluster furniture for activities and use fabric, floor covering, and paint for unity. In New Orleans, Laurie introduced visual flow in a kitchen/dining/living area using paint, a sisal rug, and yellow and green slipcovers or new upholstery for all the furniture.

Molding Character

STYLE LESSON: Shape a classic with moldings.
BACKGROUND: Even with a high ceiling, this spacious master bedroom lacks personality. Doug decides to design heavenly digs steeped in traditional style. He uses moldings to instantly infuse the room with dynamic, dimensional appeal.

Visit Another Dimension ◄

Glaze always gives walls a look of depth; moldings add still more dimension. Doug gives this voluminous space more interest as well as an air of intimacy by adding crown molding to rim the room about a foot above the windows. On the walls, narrower moldings form rectangular panels for more architectural interest; the rectangles serve as beautiful frames for candle sconces. Painting all the moldings white makes them stand out.

Medium gray paint applied above the crown molding and on the ceiling adds a sense of warmth to the room while suggesting a velvety night sky.

Wrapped in Tranquillity ◄

Though the homeowners originally envisioned their bedroom dressed in earth tones, they were delighted with the ethereal blue color-wash finish Doug selected. Three shades of blue glaze are randomly brushed over a blue base coat to achieve the soft, serene effect. "Don't overanalyze how you apply the paint," Doug says. "Just get in there, brush it on, and don't think about it."

Before 2.13.2

A high ceiling and generous floor space earn high marks with the owners of this master bedroom, but they're tired of white walls and wimpy character.

For faux-painting ideas and tools, visit a paint store or the paint department in a home center. You may also find free publications chock-full of instructions. Also, see pages 40 and 41 for more tools and techniques.

Weathered and Wonderful ▲

Though lovely, the existing cherry wood furnishings seemed too dark for the soft-blue tranquil setting. A white base coat rubbed with a dark glaze gives the furniture a vintage, weathered look that fits the "Cosmo Shab" theme Doug adds. Even the hardware on the furniture receives a makeover with hammered-pewter spray paint.

Sleep on a Cloud ▲

What could be more inviting than a cloudlike comforter floating in a blue-sky setting? Doug uses small doses of black and white toile as pillows and window treatments, creating traditional elegance. The crystal-laden chandelier—another timeless touch—is borrowed from the dining room, spray-painted black, and hung above the bed to replace an ordinary fixture.

Great Glaze Guidelines
Tinted glazes give walls drama and depth.

One of the key elements to beautiful faux-painted finishes is glaze. Tinted and applied over a low-sheen base coat, glaze lends depth and dimension to ordinary flat walls because your eye travels through the semitransparent medium to the base coat below.

For easy cleanup, use water-base medium and tint it with a small amount of latex or acrylic paint. How much color to add depends on how intense you want the glaze to appear.

You can apply glaze with a number of tools, materials, and techniques to create a variety of faux finishes. Glaze dries quickly, so no matter what tools you use, keep moving and enlist a helper if needed. To create ethereal bedroom walls, use a color-wash technique:

Apply tinted glaze using light crosshatch brushstrokes randomly on the wall.

For an entirely different effect, working in small sections, roll a thin layer of glaze over a base coat on the wall; then use tools or materials to remove some of the glaze. For example, lift off glaze with a rolled-up rag or wadded plastic wrap; or drag the bristles of a large brush through glaze. To further soften the look of your chosen technique, lightly "smudge" over your still-wet special effect with a damp sponge or a soft, dry brush.

Before beginning your project, experiment with your technique on a scrap piece of drywall or on poster board.

Nifty Faux-Painting Tools

Stroll the aisles of home centers, crafts stores, and paint stores and you'll likely come across faux-painting supplies to create a beautiful finish.

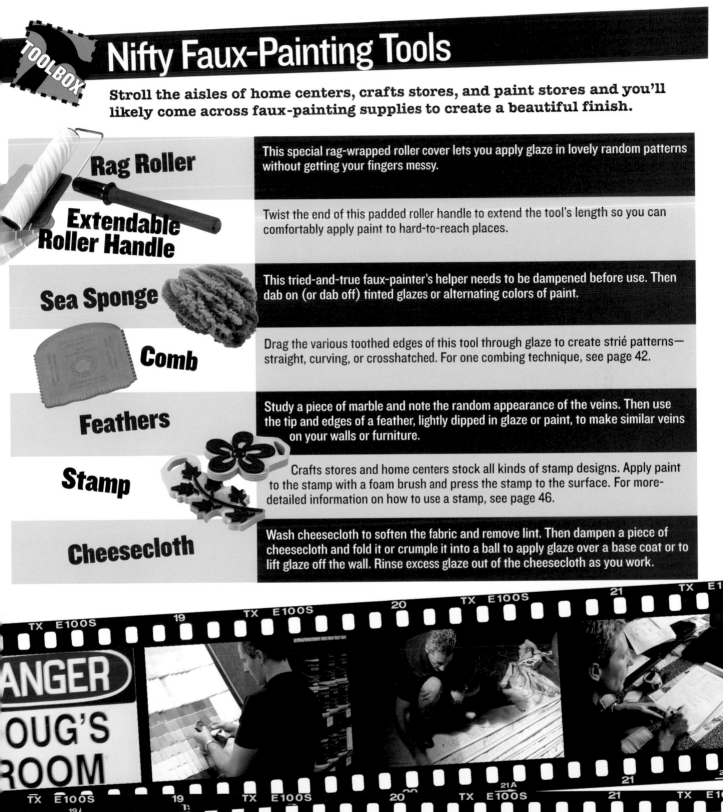

Rag Roller — This special rag-wrapped roller cover lets you apply glaze in lovely random patterns without getting your fingers messy.

Extendable Roller Handle — Twist the end of this padded roller handle to extend the tool's length so you can comfortably apply paint to hard-to-reach places.

Sea Sponge — This tried-and-true faux-painter's helper needs to be dampened before use. Then dab on (or dab off) tinted glazes or alternating colors of paint.

Comb — Drag the various toothed edges of this tool through glaze to create strié patterns—straight, curving, or crosshatched. For one combing technique, see page 42.

Feathers — Study a piece of marble and note the random appearance of the veins. Then use the tip and edges of a feather, lightly dipped in glaze or paint, to make similar veins on your walls or furniture.

Stamp — Crafts stores and home centers stock all kinds of stamp designs. Apply paint to the stamp with a foam brush and press the stamp to the surface. For more-detailed information on how to use a stamp, see page 46.

Cheesecloth — Wash cheesecloth to soften the fabric and remove lint. Then dampen a piece of cheesecloth and fold it or crumple it into a ball to apply glaze over a base coat or to lift glaze off the wall. Rinse excess glaze out of the cheesecloth as you work.

Fun Faux Techniques

Faux-finish walls, furniture, floors, doors—even the ceiling!

This trio of faux-painting strategies can help you enliven walls, furniture, or floors with textural finishes created from ordinary paint and glaze.

Creative Combing

Paint on a base coat; let dry. Tint glaze with desired color. Roll on a strip of glaze and immediately drag the combing tool down the wall in one continuous motion. Wipe glaze from comb; then repeat the steps as you move across the wall.

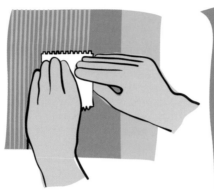
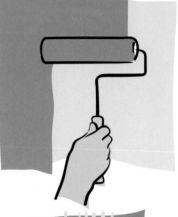

Glorious Wood Grain

Choose two tones of the same color of latex paint—one dark and one light. Use the lighter tone for the base coat; let dry. Tint glaze with the darker tone. Roll a narrow, vertical strip of glaze onto the surface. Pull a graining tool down the strip of glaze. Rock the graining tool forward and backward as you pull downward. Work quickly to create the texture before the glaze dries. Remove excess glaze from the graining tool with a rag. As you work on the next strip of glaze, slightly overlap the graining effect. If necessary, soften the grain lines by lightly dabbing the pattern and overlap lines with a slightly damp rag or a dry brush.

Lovely Linen

Choose two tones of the same color of latex paint—one dark and one light. Use the lighter tone for the base coat; let dry. Tint glaze with the darker tone. Roll glaze over a 4-foot-square section of the wall. Immediately pull a linen-technique brush (available at home centers or paint stores) horizontally through the glaze. Pull the brush back over the same pass in the opposite direction. Quickly repeat the technique to cover the 4-foot section. Wipe excess glaze from brush. Lightly brush vertically, with downward strokes, over the 4-foot section. Repeat steps to cover wall.

For an optional tea-stain finish, tint additional glaze with golden-brown paint. Use a clean, lint-free rag to lightly rub the glaze over the faux linen.

Just Faux You

Creating different looks with paints, glazes, and special tools is a lot of fun. Let these looks inspire you to experiment with your own painterly approaches.

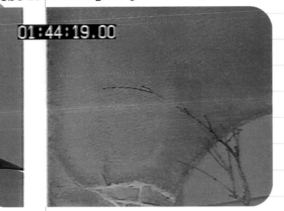

Mix in some texture. Supplement latex wall paint with sand, pebbles, or straw to create a custom wall-finishing product. When the paint dries, the additives remain stuck to the walls, producing rustic, random texture. Frank textured the walls of a Mediterranean-style living room in Ft. Lauderdale: 59th Street by mixing sand with paint and sponging it onto the walls.

Take a cue from nature. Suede, grass, leather—let natural materials such as these inspire your faux surface treatment. Laurie painted a faux-tortoiseshell border on a coffee table top in a Miami living room. She brushed a mixture of malt vinegar, pigment, and dishwashing liquid over a base coat of ivory and then tapped her fingers in the wet finish.

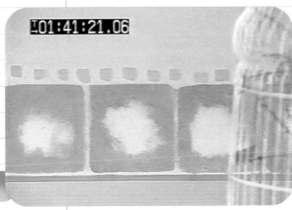

Sponge on some interest. To create shapes with glaze, use household sponges and wide paintbrushes. Frank painted a faux-tile backsplash in a Chicago kitchen, using a household sponge cut into a square. He dipped the sponge in orange paint and used it to stamp a row of orange squares. To apply the smaller row of squares, he used a wide paintbrush.

Mimic stone. Use specialty spray paints, or glazes and paints, to give surfaces the look of authentic stone, such as granite or marble. In Long Island: Steuben Boulevard, Edward painted a dresser top and sconces to mimic malachite. To a dry gray-green basecoat, Edward applied green crafts paint mixed with an extender additive. He dragged a torn piece of card stock through the wet top layer to form overlapping, wavy circular fan patterns.

Glaze over a painted wall. Paint the walls a desired color and let dry. Apply glaze and use cheesecloth, paper bags, or specialty tools to remove portions of glaze. In Austin: Wing Road, Hildi painted glaze over existing yellow walls and then patted the surface with large pieces of crumpled plastic sheeting.

East Indian Opulence

STYLE LESSON: Borrow classic designs from other cultures. **BACKGROUND:** Though India and a purple petunia seem to have nothing in common, Frank used both as his inspiration in creating a timeless look for this master bedroom. Lavish, silky fabrics and deep colors capture the flavor of the Far East.

Meditative Touches ◀

Inspired by styles from colonial India, Frank designs a lavish look for a bedroom makeover. To bring in "velvety opulence," he uses the petals of a petunia as a guide in choosing smoky purple paint for the walls. The rich color sets a sultry stage for abundant, luxurious fabrics, such as a richly patterned bedspread and shams and armloads of silky beaded pillows. Framing the headboard as an alluring focal point, a lush, gathered crown of purple-red fabric cascades down the wall. Frank reworks the existing window valances and stencils on a gold Indian-style design. Side tables fashioned from rattan wastebaskets are topped with glossy black tiles to continue the exotic look. *To learn how to stencil and stamp designs, see page 46.*

Cabinet Creation ▶

After topping an existing dresser with this cabinet, Frank painted both a deep purple-burgundy with oyster-shell white trim. New wrought iron handles complete the transformation.

Lavish Lamp ▼

Frank gave the ho-hum lampshades much needed makeovers with pretty patterned fabric, satin cording, and beaded trim.

45

Dressed-Up Designs ▶

Frank gives a basic louvered cabinet door more personality by stenciling on this glam design using metallic gold paint. Stenciling brings painted pattern into a room; stamping offers a fun alternative method. You'll find a wide variety of stamps and stencil supplies at crafts stores.

Stamp and Stencil
Two techniques to embellish surfaces

If painting designs freehand isn't your thing, you'll love these easy techniques and the great results that each offers.

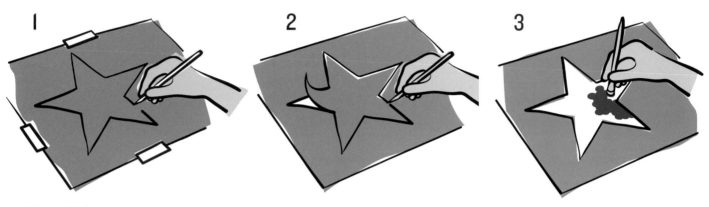

1   2   3

Stencil Away

1 **Place a sheet of tracing paper over your stencil** pattern. Trace the pattern with a pencil. Use transfer paper and a stylus to transfer your pattern to stencil acetate or stenciling film.

2 **Lay the transferred design on a cutting board** and cut the outline areas of each piece. For better control, always pull the crafts knife toward you when cutting.

3 **Use quick-release painter's tape** or spray the stencil with adhesive; then press the stencil into place on the surface. Load the stencil brush with a small amount of paint and tap or wipe off most of the paint on a paper towel. Move the brush gently in a circle or with a light tapping motion to fill in the stencil. Carefully lift the stencil off the surface.

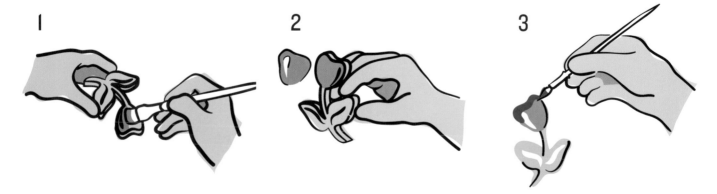

1   2   3

Stamp Some Style

1 **Apply paint to the stamp with a flat brush** using a blotting motion. To determine the right amount of paint, experiment by stamping the design on paper.

2 **Evenly press the stamp on the wall** or surface you're embellishing. Lift the stamp straight off. If necessary, touch up the stamped area with a flat brush.

3 **To add dimension to the stamped design,** dilute the paint with water to an inky consistency. Use a round brush to add colorful details.

Make It Yours: Lamps and Shades

You might do a double take when you learn that each of these projects begins with the same wood lamp base and plain white shade. Easy embellishment makes each one a personal statement. Take a look at these ideas and dream up your own custom look.

Beaded Beauty

Paint lampshade with crafts paint that coordinates with the bead color of your choice. Or use spray paint. Let dry. Working in small sections and using a foam brush, apply decoupage medium to the lampshade and pour 8- to 10-mm seed beads over medium. Tap beads with fingers to level beads and ensure they stick. Let dry for a couple of minutes and then gently lift and shake the shade to allow excess beads to fall off. After the shade is covered and all beads have dried, use hot glue to attach beaded trim or other decorative fabric finish to the inside of the bottom shade seam. Paint lamp base as desired with coordinating acrylic crafts paint. Attach bands of narrow satin ribbon or other decorative trim with hot glue to create decorative bands of color on the painted base.

Fun with Fabric

Select a fabric that has a motif with simple lines. Cut out the motifs with sharp scissors, trimming directly on the outline, or leaving some of the background fabric as shown. Apply spray adhesive to the backs of the motifs, positioning them as desired on the lampshade. Cut out additional fabric motifs for the lamp base. Punch a hole in the center of each motif with a small-diameter crafts punch and string the motifs onto a length of plastic crafts lace in a complementary color. Tie the loose end of the crafts lace to the top of the lamp base. Wind the lace around the base, positioning the fabric motifs for a three-dimensional look. When the entire base is covered, cut the lace and adhere to the bottom of the lamp base with a small piece of transparent tape; cover the tape with a fabric motif.

Desert Drama

To embellish the shade, cut semitransparent art papers into the desired shapes and sizes. Brush the backs of the art papers with decoupage medium or water-thinned white glue using a foam brush and press papers to shade, randomly overlapping the papers as desired. Let dry. Tie together short pieces of leather lacing to form bands around the top and bottom of the shade. Randomly tie additional leather laces around the lamp base, securing pieces of lace with a few dots of hot glue as needed. Set the lamp in a large terra-cotta saucer, positioning the lamp base off center; attach lamp base to saucer with hot glue. Hot-glue a piece of florist's foam to the saucer. Press silk or plastic succulents and cactus into the florist's foam. Fill entire terra-cotta saucer with smooth river pebbles.

Soft and Shimmery

Lightly sand wood lamp base to remove glossy finish. Use premixed ceramic tile adhesive and grout to set and grout small objects on the base, such as broken ceramic tiles, mirror tiles, marbles, or glass florist's pebbles. Apply adhesive to the backs of objects with a putty knife. Press the objects onto the lamp base. Wipe off excess adhesive. After covering the base, allow adhesive to dry according to manufacturer's directions, usually about 24 hours. Press grout between objects with your fingers or a crafts stick. (Wear rubber gloves.) Wipe away excess with a damp sponge and polish off haze with a soft, dry cloth. To finish shade, cut a length of chiffon fabric. Gather fabric around top of shade first, creating folds, and secure to the inside of the shade with a cool-melt glue gun. Secure bottom edge of fabric to inside bottom edge of shade with the cool-melt glue gun.

WHY BE SHY?

Chapter 3: Why Be Shy? Be brave and explore uncharted territory in design. Each of these rooms basks in the limelight like a performer on the stage, boasting a decor that's like no other. Take a look because you might just discover an exciting new way to live.

¡¡WELCOME HOME BABY!!

50

One Powerful Color

They will be able to party in this room!

STYLE LESSON: Use one bold color for impact.
BACKGROUND: Even the most humdrum room can become a sensation. Gen shows how with deep red paint on all the walls and the ceiling. Crisp white trim and sleek lighted shelves introduce architectural pizzazz.

Lavished in Red ◄

Because this room enjoys plenty of natural light from nice-size windows, Gen confidently dresses the walls in sultry, deepest red paint, knowing it will yield dramatic results. "Red paint requires the most pigment," she points out, "so do three coats." (When painting a room in deep color, plan to apply two to three coats to cover old color.) Window treatments and a few pillows feature bigger-than-life floral motifs reminiscent of fabric designs from the 1940s. (See "Fun with Bark Cloth," page 53.)

Beauty and the Bargains ▼

Painting the ceiling the same color as the walls and adding white crown molding creates dramatic contrast; commonplace molding becomes a knockout decorative element. Door and window casings in crisp white also lend an appealing dash of "uncolor" amid the deep, luxurious red. Gen found a number of other bargains to fill out the room. The white chair and couch, for example, are plucked from the homeowners' garage—a structure so packed to the rafters with goodies that Gen exclaimed, "This is a furniture store!" For artwork, she cut out photographs from a book and frames the images.

51

light." Clear sealer lets the light color of the wood show; the wood itself adds a warm element. *To learn more about basic wood cube construction, such as these bottle display shelves, turn to page 148.*

The Dining Connection ▲

Embracing the same color palette for the adjoining dining area solidifies the power of the approach. For subtle variety, the walls are ever so slightly lighter in this area, but the bark cloth fabric on the chair seats and at the window creates continuity. New paint coats the chairs as well as the secretary cabinet in the corner, which now serves as a minibar. The glossy black used for the chairs pulls accent color from the windows to the middle of the room. White moldings add bright contrast, as they do in the living room, but a trio of lighted display shelves commands the most attention.

Shelf Expectancy ▲

To display a collection of bottles, Gen uses these simple wood boxes—each topped with a sheet of translucent acrylic and lighted from below with fluorescent tubes to set the colorful bottles aglow. "With all the dark color on the walls," Gen says, "I needed to break it up with something

52

Fun with Bark Cloth

Use vintage-design fabrics for more character and color.

In the 1940s and 1950s, homeowners dressed rooms in matching draperies, pillows, bedspreads, and upholstered furniture—all done in a pebbly textured fabric called bark cloth. No shrinking violet, bark cloth makes its presence known in any room: Typically bold patterns run the gamut from cabbage roses to cowboys to tropical florals to feathers. The bold look of bark cloth means you don't need much of it to make a statement; Gen uses it stylishly here with a few dashes at the windows and on pillows. Watch for bark cloth bargains at garage sales, flea markets, and online auctions. The fabrics are fun to collect and sprinkle around the house; for an easy display, stack the folded fabrics in colorful layers on open shelves.

Group your collections by color or subject to create a focal point. Whenever possible, vary heights for more interest; use vintage books or small painted boxes, if needed, to elevate an object.

How to Hang Anything

Ordinary drywall can safely hold a lightweight object hung from a nail; heavier objects require different anchors. Head to the hardware store for solutions.

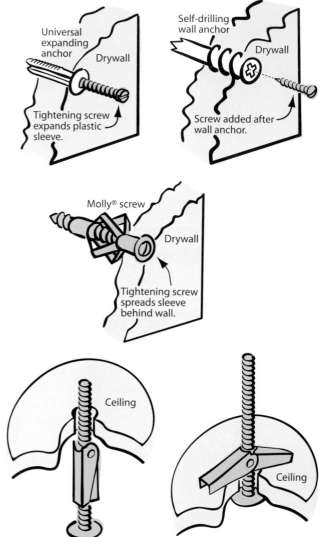

Put down the putty and poster tacks—that's no way to hang a gorgeous mirror or framed artwork. Whenever you can, hang these items from a nail or screw driven directly into a wall stud. Of course, you might not want all your arrangements rigidly spaced 16 inches on-center. So when you know you won't hit a stud, hit the hardware store instead and gather up a good selection of these nifty hollow-wall anchors. (They also work when you want to hang something from the ceiling, such as shelves suspended from eye screws and chains.)

Universal expanding anchor. To hang lighter objects on drywall, plaster, or masonry, use this plastic anchor with a variety of screw sizes. Drill a hole that's slightly smaller than the anchor and insert the anchor. Then drive in a sheet metal screw to hold the object.

Self-drilling wall anchor. Intended for drywall only, a self-drilling wall anchor should be driven directly into the wall with a screwdriver or drill. Then drive in the screw. This anchor holds light- to heavyweight objects.

Molly bolt. Look for self-tapping Molly bolts with a pointed tip so you can drive this screw-and-sleeve device into drywall. (Don't use these on plaster.) As you tighten the screw, the sleeve expands behind the wall to hold the screw in place. Use this anchor for moderate-weight objects.

Toggle bolt. Pass the folded wings of a toggle bolt through a hole you've predrilled. As you tighten the bolt, the wings spread out behind the wall. Use toggle bolts for moderate-weight objects on drywall or plaster or for heavyweight objects on hollow-core concrete block.

TOOLBOX
Cordless Drills
No cords to trip over; no extensions to tangle up in knots

Cordless drills may be one of the handiest tools on the market. You can tote them anywhere around the house or yard and not have to worry whether the extension cord is long enough. Depending on how you equip your drill, you can drill holes of almost any size or use it to drive screws. You'll probably get the most use out of a ⅜-inch or ½-inch drill. (That dimension indicates the size of shank on the bit, not the size of hole you can drill.) Invest in high-speed steel bits because they last longer. When appropriate, use bits specially designed to drill through specific materials, such as metal, concrete, china, and wood. Purchase a cordless drill set with two battery packs so you can charge one while you're using the other.

Shelf Expressions

Give books, photographs, and knickknacks a stylish home.

Shelves can be more than ordinary rectangular surfaces. Take the road less traveled by designing shelves with unique style, such as these.

Invest in fine details. Build a shelving unit out of inexpensive materials such as plywood or MDF; then apply fine details—wood molding, fabulous faux paint, or wood veneer. In Ft. Lauderdale: 59th Street, Hildi hung large interlocking rectangles as display shelves for a dish collection. Ty built the shelves with inexpensive MDF and ironed on wood veneer fronts.

Incorporate paint and tape. If you want the look of an expansive wall unit, but don't have the time or money to build dozens of shelves and supports, combine your shelf with decorative paint details. In a living room in Orlando, Laurie balanced oddly placed wall insets and a collection of various-sized shelves by taping off rectangles and applying a coat of coordinating paint.

Claim unused space. Look around a space and pinpoint areas that aren't being used to their full potential. Cathedral ceilings, areas above and below windows, and nooks and crannies are all candidates for custom storage makeovers. Laurie took advantage of limited space in Houston: Sawdust Street by building an open shelving unit that went up and over the sofa.

Look for circular solutions. Lazy-Susans work well in kitchen cabinets, so extend this helpful design feature to other storage areas. Place cabinets or end tables on revolving platforms or lay out shelving in circular orientations to allow for 360 degrees of use. In Seattle: 56th Place, Gen built shelves that mimic the 360-degree design of a circular staircase.

Mix pipe and board. Personalize the classic shelving combo of pipe and board by selecting the perfect pipe (such as PVC or copper) and board (such as pine or oak). In an office/playroom, Laurie combined black-painted planks and silver plumbing conduit into a desk/shelving unit.

The homeowners—Washington, D.C., newlyweds—say their bedroom needs a headboard and some personality too. They're hoping for a redo that's sophisticated, contemporary, and sexy—all rolled into one.

Before 7.17

Groomed for Glamour

STYLE LESSON: Glass and metal add sparkle to a bold palette.
BACKGROUND: Vern adds a dramatic headboard with silken insets, installs shimmering metal and glass accents, and delivers punches of bold color to transform this Washington, D.C., bedroom into a glamorous getaway.

Focal-Point Finesse ◀

Vern matches paint color to elegant red silk that he purchased overseas for a bargain and transforms the fireplace into a brilliant focal point—simply by painting the brick facade vibrant red. Restful taupe for the surrounding walls serves as a subtle and classic backdrop that allows the fireplace and a new 8-foot-wide headboard to stand out. The custom-made headboard combines a glossy black frame and a series of red silk insets that offer softness and dimension. At the foot of the bed, the color scheme continues with a pair of storage chests topped with red cushions for seating. Overhead, a pendant light fixture with a red shade replaces the less-inspiring ceiling fan.

Underfoot, hardwood floors that were formerly hidden by carpet now wear a red area rug for color and warmth.

Let It Shine ▼

Building your own headboard makes introducing special features easier. Vern found four chrome downlights to install above the bed. The cords run behind the headboard, out of sight. The lights are practical for reading and add eye-pleasing shine to the room.

Multiple Magic ◀

Instead of choosing a painting or other traditional artwork for the bedroom, Vern opts for these glistening rows of individual crystals, which hang from wire and narrow metal rods. Below this sparkling sculpture, clear glass gobletlike votives line up atop the mantel to add the glow of candlelight to the upper portion of the fireplace.

57

Comforting
Ideas ◀

Allover delicate red
designs give the
pristine white linen duvet
simple, uncomplicated style.
The milky color of the linen makes the red sheets and
pillows appear even bolder and more dramatic. A
duvet, which slips over a comforter like a pillowcase, is
easily removed for cleaning and offers a fast and
affordable way to change the look and
color palette of a bedroom with the
seasons—or on a whim!

Dressing in Style ▲

Vern creates balance by carrying the red to this
dressing and closet area opposite the fireplace. The
space features an attractive arched niche fitted with a
dressing table. "The red anchors the room," Vern says.
"The stone color in the middle keeps it nice and
serene." New contemporary chrome pulls update the
closet doors. Vern introduces some shimmer to this end
of the room by stylishly lining the niche with
affordable mirrored tiles that brighten the space by
reflecting light. Applying dark stain to the chairs helps
unify them with other furniture. Linen fabric on the
chair cushions complements the comforter.

Bureau Chief ◀

Sometimes the *Trading Spaces* designers must build an entire armoire from scratch, but Vern cleverly customizes an existing piece to realize the benefits of an armoire for less time and money. To put the television under wraps, a new cabinet tops the chest of drawers. For unity, the upper cabinet features the same pulls as the closet doors in the dressing area. Red silk insets in the cabinet doors match the fabric insets on the headboard. The Roman shade at the window and the lampshade nearby also boast the same red silk fabric.

TOOLBOX

Jigsaw   This handy tool makes cutting shapes easy.

A jigsaw—sometimes called a saber saw—can cut straight lines like a circular saw (though not as fast), but it's most prized for its light weight and ability to cut curves. Low-power, corded jigsaws start at about $30, but you can spend hundreds of dollars or more on sophisticated high-power, cordless models. Look for one with a motor that's 3 amps or higher; check that the model is designed for easy blade changes. Purchase the right blades for the job—some work best cutting straight lines, curves, or bevels. Specific blades can also cut through metal, veneer, ceramic, masonry, and even leather or plastic. To make accurate straight cuts, clamp a piece of 1× lumber atop the material you plan to cut and align the 1× parallel to the mark but spaced to allow for the width of the saw plate. Make curved cuts freehand or follow a template precut from tempered hardboard.

Pillow Talk ◄

Floral appliqués make the plain red silk pillows on the bed even prettier. To add appliqués such as these to existing plain pillows, cut a fabric panel to any size and shape, centering a design in the middle if you wish. Leave ½ inch all the way around for folding under. Turn the allowance under and press with an iron. Use a needle and matching thread to whipstitch the appliqué in place.

For more ideas on embellishing purchased pillows, turn to page 17.

Sew a Bolster
Bolster the beauty of your bedroom or living room with these tube-shape pillows.

A custom bolster is a great way to add variety and color to the room. Create a custom bolster—as long or short and as thick or thin as you want. Follow these basic steps:

1 **Cut fabric to the desired width;** cut length according to the finished circumference of the bolster. Be sure to add 1 inch to the overall width and length for ½-inch seam allowances.

2 **Bring the short ends of the fabric together and form a tube shape** (with the right side of the fabric inside the tube); pin and stitch the side seam with a ½-inch allowance.

3 **Cut circular end pieces with ½-inch seam allowances.** Sew piping or other trim to each circular end piece; snip notches all around ends and also on the bolster tube allowances.

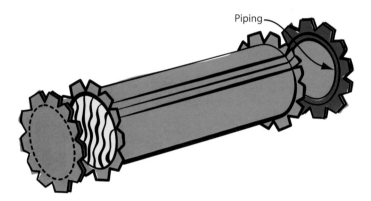

Piping

4 **Align raw edges of the bolster tube and end pieces** and pin in place. Sew pieces together but leave a small opening for turning and stuffing. Turn the bolster cover right side out; stuff with fiberfill or a pillow form. Hand-sew the opening closed.

Worth the Rescue?
Questions to ask before investing time and money

When you're considering whether to keep a piece of furniture to fix up or slipcover, use these guidelines to decide if it's worth the effort:

✱ **Is it sturdy?** Shake the furniture to see if it wobbles. If it's a chair and you sink when you sit, it could be a major project.

✱ **Do you love the lines?** Consider what you like and don't like about the look of the piece. For storage pieces, do you like the design of the legs, drawers, and doors? If it's a seating piece, what do you think of the arms, the back, and the legs?

✱ **Is it comfortable?** For seating pieces, you can add a little extra padding before slipcovering, but you can't significantly change the way the piece fits or supports your body. (To learn more about slipcovering, turn to page 36.)

✱ **Is it worth the money?** Even if you're doing the labor, consider how much money you'll have to invest in the piece to achieve the desired look.

Fireplace Fix-Ups

The hearth is a natural focal point, but sometimes your fireplace needs a nudge to take center stage. Fire up your decorating strategies with these hot ideas.

Go faux. Use decorative painting techniques, wood trim, tile, or brick facing to mimic the look of bricks, marble, or architectural designs. In a Cincinnati living room, Frank framed pieces of textured wallpaper with decorative lumber and then brushed on black antiquing medium to enhance the faux-tin look.

Encase for a complete makeover. Love your fireplace but hate its look? Enclose the original fireplace surround with a boxlike screen of plywood. Paint and finish with decorative trim that better suits your look. In Seattle: I37th Street, Doug infamously built a removable wood "fireplace slipcover" that encased the fireplace in crisp white plywood and trim.

Tile in style. For a clean, chic look, cover the hearth and surrounding fireplace wall with ceramic, stone, wood, or other tile. Extend an unimpressive fireplace up to the ceiling with this technique. In a Texas living room, Hildi attached lightly stained wood squares with an alternating grain pattern to the area around a stone fireplace.

Take your fireplace to new heights. Construct a wood frame, attach custom-built pillars, apply a decorative paint technique, or hang large-scale artwork or a mirror above a fireplace to pull the eye high. In an Indianapolis living room, Doug accentuated the ceiling height by extending the wood trim design above the original fireplace and adding a large-scale mirror.

Make the fireplace part of a unit. Add bookcases, wall shelving, or a special wall treatment to each side of a fireplace, creating a symmetrical, dramatic focal wall. In Gen's basement family room, Ty installed simple pine bookshelves on either side of a fireplace, building a multipurpose wall unit in the process.

Before

White walls, a mattress on a metal frame, and beer cooler nightstands signal that this Las Vegas bedroom is definitely ready for a redo.

Impromptu Four-Poster

Doug takes ordinary to surprising places!

STYLE LESSON: Unexpected materials and finishes make a statement.
BACKGROUND: Doug has fun using poles in this bedroom, but these metal elements bring serious structure to an ordinary space. A special wall treatment, moldings, and a round armoire create a one-of-a-kind retreat.

Sleeping Beauty ◀

Home centers and other suppliers are loaded with materials you can use in surprising ways. Doug uses decidedly nontraditional materials to design an unusual four-poster bed for this Las Vegas bedroom. Four metal poles—you know, the kind exotic dancers, um, use—figure into the equation. With one pole stationed at each corner of the bed, the mattress and box spring on a standard metal frame become a substantial focal point that's loaded with contemporary style. Around the top of each pole, molding frames add stability and easy architectural appeal. Rich brown and royal blue bedding—including a plush brown velvet comforter—make the bed luxurious.

Well-Rounded Design ▶

The new armoire features an unusual

round cabinet that sits atop a pedestal. Brown half-moon panels and long, graceful silver handles on the doors unite the white-painted armoire with other furnishings in the bedroom. Though this armoire is built from scratch, you could fashion something similar using an old redwood hot tub that's cut down in depth and mounted on a pedestal of your own design.

Beside the armoire, a reupholstered thrift store armchair offers a comfortable seat for reading. The pillow is brown velvet with a snazzy blue wave down the center. Simple blue fabric panels on the windows suit the new decor.

Doug introduces an abundance of white accents, which prevent the deep brown walls and intense blue fabrics from overpowering the room. The contrast between light and dark makes this a dramatic space.

Showstoppers ▲

A Venetian plaster finish gives the walls a leather look. After priming the walls dark brown, the neighbors used trowels to apply three very thin coats of a brown-tinted compound. They sanded between coats and used a finish coat of buffed wax to make the walls smooth and shiny. On the ceiling, a salmon hue prevents the room from appearing too dark. White-painted crown moldings, which match the moldings that top the poles, stand out against the dark hues and give the room still more structure.

Paint unifies the brand-new dresser with a pair of nightstands that Doug found at a thrift store. White paint for the furniture frames, brown for the drawer fronts, and new silvery hardware meld the storage pieces with the new look of the room.

To give the homeowners much-needed lighting, Doug opts for two different pairs of lamps—one set with shining silver bases and another with elegant frosted-glass bases.

Rescue and Reuse

Be creative with castoffs and transform trash into treasure.

About the time you think something in your home is on its last leg, someone comes along and figures out how to make it usable. The *Trading Spaces* designers do this with thrift store and salvage yard finds all the time. Here are a few ideas to get you started thinking of new uses for ordinary objects:

✳ Lay an old door atop a new base (or screw on purchased turned legs) and create a dining table.

✳ Old iron floor grates with intricate designs become interesting artwork on the wall. Or set a grate on a base and top it with glass to serve as an occasional table.

✳ Employ architectural corbels as shelf brackets.

✳ Hang an old wooden ladder parallel to the kitchen ceiling and above the range as a rustic pot rack.

✳ Salvage vintage multipane window sashes and use them to frame artwork or three-dimensional objects.

✳ Cut the legs off an old table to make a low coffee table.

✳ Use old linoleum to make a floorcloth. Cut the piece to the desired size and shape. Prime; let dry. Paint, stencil, and decorate as desired using latex paints; let dry. Protect with several coats of polyurethane.

✳ Salvage old boxes, baskets, and other vessels and use them as unusual containers for bouquets. Simply slip a waterproof liner, such as a plastic bowl, inside the container and add flowers and water.

Watch the curbsides, alleys, and ditches for true castoffs. You might be surprised by some of the stuff people decide to toss!

Cutting Miters

Smooth angle cuts and tight-fitting mitered corners make projects look professional.

Although a miter box is handy for cutting smaller pieces of wood, you need another strategy for cutting larger lumber and plywood. Take a look at these two techniques:

A

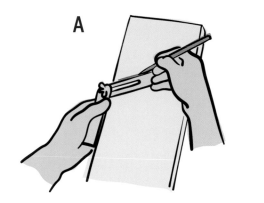

B

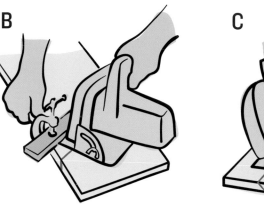

C

1 **Align a T bevel to the desired angle** and mark the angle on the wood as shown (A). C-clamp a straight piece of 1× lumber atop the piece you plan to cut, aligning the 1× with the marked line. Use the 1× as a cutting guide for a circular saw or jigsaw (B). Allow space between the cutting guide and the marked line to match the distance between the saw blade and the edge of the base plate on the saw.

2 **To make a bevel cut with a circular saw,** mark the cutting line with a straightedge. On the edge of the material you plan to cut, mark the angle. Adjust the circular saw to match that angle. (Use the T bevel tool to double-check the angle of the saw against the angle you marked on the edge of the wood.) Clamp a 1× parallel to the mark, allowing for the width of the base plate on the saw. Make the cut by guiding the saw blade along the cutoff line (C).

When using a miter box, place a scrap of 1×4 in the bottom first so you can saw through the molding without cutting into the bottom of the miter box. To avoid confusion, place the board or molding in the position it will occupy when in use.

TOOLBOX

Miter Box
Plastic or wood, a miter box is inexpensive.

To make angle, or miter, cuts in narrow pieces of wood or moldings, use a miter box—a simple device that holds a backsaw at the proper angle while you saw. If there's any trick at all to using a miter box, it's not in the technique of cutting, but in correctly measuring and marking for the cut. To make sure you don't cut the piece too short or angle it the wrong way, draw a rough sketch before you begin, showing how the pieces will fit together. Then position the wood piece against the side of the miter box that's farthest from you, position the backsaw as needed to make the correct cut, and hold the end of the wood piece in place with your free hand. Push and pull the backsaw back and forth to cut through the wood piece.

Molding Magic

Think of moldings as style on the straight and narrow.

Use molding as a frame. Create your own custom frames from molding. Have a home center or frame shop cut molding to the required dimensions—or cut it yourself with a backsaw and miter box. In a Maryland bedroom, Doug painted Matisse-inspired figures on the wall and made them look like hung artwork by installing molding around the paintings.

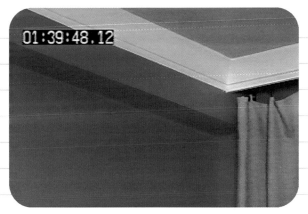

01:39:48.12

Employ molding as fool-the-eye technique. Details draw the eye's attention. Introduce molding strategically into a space to pull attention away from less attractive aspects of a room—or to highlight attractive features. In a bedroom in London: Garden Flat, Gen added crown moldings to disguise an odd wall jog that hid pipes in the ceiling.

01:44:18.04

Create drama with molding. Boost the design impact of molding and trim by enlarging the thickness or depth of the molding. Add molding to existing trim or replace diminutive trim with larger-scale options. In Plano: Shady Valley Road, Hildi added 12-inch orange baseboards to a cathedral ceiling bedroom in order to draw the eye down to floor level.

01:40:38.10

Add crowning touches with molding. Stock cabinetry, ready-to-assemble furniture, and flea market finds gain style when you attach wood trim or medallions. Doug added crown molding to the top of existing kitchen cabinets to give them a more finished look.

TCR 01:40.26:03
PLAY   LOCK

Form furniture with molding. Going beyond embellishments, some moldings are substantial enough to serve as furniture. Combine trims to create custom shelving, seating, and storage. In San Diego, Frank wanted a dramatic headboard without the bulk and expense of a new piece of furniture. He attached wide molding to the wall to resemble a fluted, classical headboard.

Chapter 4: Come On Over Maybe you want a room to look and function for entertaining a host of friends. Or perhaps you are just longing for ways to make spaces seem as inviting as a front porch swing. Whichever goal is yours, you'll find cozy features and styles for every room....

COME ON OVER

69

Magical Madrid

STYLE LESSON: Curves and touchable textures welcome everyone. **BACKGROUND:** A stately old-world Spanish decor evolves as Laurie orchestrates an inviting dining room, combining shapely metal furnishings with a focal point wall of wide leatherlike strips.

Wake Up the Walls ◄

To make this dining room an attractive space where everyone will want to gather, Laurie combined elements characteristic of old-world Spain: terra-cotta tiles, brown leather, and skillfully crafted black wrought iron. By painting the walls terra-cotta, she provides a subtle backdrop for more-dramatic features, such as a focal point wall layered in wide, woven strips of a leather look-alike.

Curve Appeal ◄

Existing chairs with distinctive black-iron spiral backs inspire this custom-made dining table in the round. The 4-foot diameter is perfect for an intimate dinner for two—or up to four good friends. The floor-length fabric table skirt—with its terra-cotta and buttery yellow quatrefoil motif—inspired the octagon and diamond stencils used to embellish the white-painted tabletop. To add a skirt to a tabletop, use hook-and-loop tape so the fabric can be removed for cleaning. Secure the adhesive-back half of the tape to the backside of the table lip. Stitch the other half to the front top edge of the skirt. Press the two halves of the tape together to secure the skirt.

The homeowners tell Laurie they want their dining room to be more inviting than it is now. Some exciting international flavor would be ideal.

To make a fabric table skirt easily removable for washing, use hook-and-loop tape to attach it to the back of the tabletop edge.

Simple Style ▲

Creating small focal points around a room—or high on the walls to direct attention upward—can be as simple as this modest arrangement. These ironstone dishes—pottery pieces that work well with the Spanish theme—look more important with a pair of corbel shelves and mounted above a carved mirror frame.

Higher Learning ▲

When you want the look to be grand, pour your limited budget into a few extra yards of fabric. Laurie took these window panels to the ceiling line, for example, emphasizing the dramatic height of the ceiling. A black iron rod and black clip-on rings keep the look in sync with the old-world theme.

The Perfect Light ▲

To transport your dining room to another place and time, include lighting that adds authenticity to your theme. This wrought-iron wonder includes candlelike luminaries and a rustic metal frame and chains painted in black.

A Motif Worth Repeating ▲

Borrowed from the existing dining chair backs, the spiral design reappears on the black-painted iron pipe base of the console-style buffet table. A fresh, clean-lined design such as this one fits vintage or contemporary styles.

Buffet Beauty ▲

Every dining room needs a landing spot for overflow serving dishes or a surface that allows buffet-style entertaining. A simple console table like this one requires few materials—in this case, a painted wood top and metal piping for the base. Ty made this base, manipulating the metal to form the graceful cabriole legs, but you can have a metal fabricator do the same thing if you don't have the tools and the skills. Look in the phone directory under "Metal Fabricators."

Thinking Themes How to keep the look comfortable and inviting— and know when to stop!

Designing a room around a theme is a terrific way to capture a look. Dream up a scheme that suits the space, such as a French bistro design for the breakfast room or a Tuscan villa for a sunroom. Jot down elements you can use to achieve the look. For a bistro look, think flirty valances, a small round table, four metal chairs, and wire and wicker baskets to hold fresh loaves of bread, produce, and colorful bouquets of fresh flowers. For a Tuscan affair, pick earthy tile, textured walls, weathered wood furniture, and wrought iron accents. You'll probably find you have more ideas than room: Remember, don't overdo the theme. Begin with a handful of elements and live with the look for a while. Gradually adding one or two features at a time makes it easier to identify when to stop.

Hammers

Get a grip on a quality, well-balanced hammer.

Visit the home center or hardware store, grip a few hammers in your hand, and you'll quickly learn what feels right and what doesn't. For most people, a 16-ounce hammer with a curved claw for extracting nails is a smart choice. If you're a smaller person or if your wrists tire easily, you might find it easier to wield a 13- or 14-ounce model. Also notice that handles come in different lengths; swing the hammer a few times to see which length is most comfortable for you. Shorter handles are good when you plan to work in close quarters. Pay attention to the material that the handle is made of. Smooth wood or a cushioned rubber coating are two options you might try out.

For upholstering furniture, hanging pictures, attaching narrow molding, and installing curtain rods and brackets, purchase a skinnier, lighter tack hammer. Also consider buying a rubber mallet—an ideal tool for adjusting a piece of molding or anything else you want to tap without damaging.

When using a hammer, grip low on the handle, as Amy Wynn is doing *above,* to ensure optimum comfort and control. Positioning your hand so high on the handle that it "chokes" the head will quickly wear out your wrist.

75

PAIGE CAM

Embellished for Beauty ◀

Details really do make a difference. Open spaces where strips intersect create dimension by allowing a glimpse of wall color. Painstaking embellishments, such as these four decorative nailheads Laurie and the homeowners applied at the corners of the openings, further enrich the woven wall. The leatherlike strips themselves lend appealing texture and offer the added benefit of edges that don't fray when cut.

Weave It Right
Use this easy weaving technique to introduce texture to all kinds of surfaces.

This easy weaving technique works as well for dressing up walls as it does for a tabletop, an armoire front, or a headboard.

Fabric isn't your only option for a weaving project. Metal flashing, paper, canvas, wire, thin wood strips, yarn, strips of rag, twine, string, or ribbon are only a few of the materials you can use to create your custom woven design. Visit a crafts store for additional ideas and have fun exploring your material options!

A Tack vertical strips in place first.

B Weave horizontal strips over and under, tacking strips in place where necessary.

Alternate ideas:

To create a wider basket-weave effect, weave horizontal strips two over and two under.

For a checkerboard effect, use different colors for vertical strips and horizontal strips.

For a softer look, embellish a woven wall by inserting dried flowers or photos between the strips.

Create a wainscoting effect on a wall by weaving material only half-way or three-quarters of the way up the wall. Finish the top edge with chair rail molding or wide ribbon.

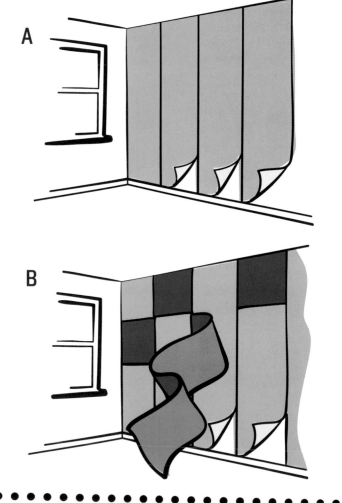

A

B

To secure ends of weaving strips to a surface, use staples and a staple gun or small nails. If the fasteners are visible, cover them with lengths of decorative cord, braiding, or ribbon secured with a glue gun. For an upholstered look, fasten ends of strips with decorative nailhead trim (see page 115).

Make It Yours: Mirrors

Identical wood-frame mirrors can take on vastly different looks when you add details using a wide range of paints and other materials. Use these ideas to get your creative juices flowing and embellish your mirror to suit your own style.

Beribboned Beauty

Spray stencil with temporary spray adhesive. Let set until tacky. Position stencil on mirror surface and burnish with fingertips to secure. Within stencil pattern, apply etching cream, following the manufacturer's directions. When etching is complete, protect glass with quick-release painter's tape and newspaper. Sand glossy finish, if any, off wood frame. Wipe with a tack cloth. Spray-paint with hammered-metal finish. Let dry. Tie wire-edge ribbon into bow. Hot-glue to frame. Twist and hot-glue ribbon ends to frame as desired. Trim ends. Hot-glue dried flower heads near bow.

Delicately Decoupage

Select decoupage paper with the desired motif. Or use motifs on other heavy papers, such as wrapping paper or greeting cards. Don't use magazine clippings because the image on the back will bleed through. Cut out the motifs. Use a foam brush to apply decoupage medium to the back of each motif and adhere to the frame and mirror. Wipe away excess decoupage medium with a damp sponge. When all motifs are in place, use a foam brush to cover entire frame with an even layer of decoupage medium. Check that motif edges are adhered to the mirror frame. Position three hooks at the bottom of the frame and screw in place.

Black Leather and Braid

Sand glossy finish. Protect glass with painter's tape and newspaper. Paint a narrow section of frame closest to the mirror with red crafts paint. Let dry. Brush on metallic leaf adhesive size; let dry until clear and tacky. Transfer leaf to sized area using tissue paper between sheets to reduce breakage. Use a soft brush to dab leaf into place. Leaf will stick only to size. Gently brush away excess leaf. Use leaf scraps to fill in missed areas, or allow some of the red base coat to show. Protect leaf with satin polyurethane. Cut and hot-glue leather to cover rest of frame. Hot-glue cording around frame as shown.

Fun and Feathery

Sand glossy finish. Paint with metallic lavender crafts paint. Let dry. Cut strips of thin crafts plastic into long triangles. Warm plastic, following manufacturer directions, and shape around fingers to form spirals. (The more times you wrap it around your fingers, the tighter the curl.) Hold spirals in place until cool—about 30 seconds. Hot-glue spirals at random angles to mirror frame. Attach feather boa to back of mirror frame by stretching it tight and pushing thumbtacks through the string that forms the center of the boa. Use dots of hot glue to finish securing slack spots.

Yep. That's a 65-inch television fighting for attention with the fireplace in this San Diego living room. The owner isn't crazy about the angled line of the chimney, and Vern says those 1970s-style vertical blinds have to go.

Before

TCR 01:42.56:10
PLAY   LOCK

Slate One Up

STYLE LESSON: Slate lends appeal.
BACKGROUND: If you ever thought you had to make do with a fireplace that doesn't suit your tastes, here's good news! Vern erased the Southwestern style of this fireplace with some clever carpentry by Amy Wynn and a stylish cover-up. A really big TV goes under wraps too.

New Style ◀

Because this is a room where a family gathers to watch television, comfort is critical. The angled chimney line and stucco facing left the homeowners feeling out of place because the decorating throughout the rest of their home did not fit the Southwestern style. Amy Wynn used framing and sheathing to square off the shape of the chimney, correcting the fireplace faux pas and creating a dramatic focal point. Vern and the neighbors gave the fireplace an entirely new appearance with a handsome facade of 12×12-inch slate tiles. To ensure a good bond for the tile mastic, one neighbor donned a face mask and used a rotating sander to scuff the painted stucco surface. To keep the tiles level and plumb, Vern then marked a grid on the wall, using a carpenter's level and a pencil. Small strips of duct tape helped prevent some of the tiles from slipping after Vern pressed them into the mastic. Adding more warmth to the room, a spiral-shape votive holder lends a soft glow above the mantel. Lots of plump pillows—some with punchy appliqués—make the room even more inviting.

The cotton chenille lined draperies were originally $119, but Vern got them on sale. The chair in the foreground is another bargain—found at a secondhand furniture store for $19. "It has a good frame and is very comfortable," Vern says, "but the fabric looked like it had been through World War III." New camel-color slipcovers for this chair and the existing sofa visually unite the two pieces. *For tips on installing tile, turn to page 82.*

79

Amy Wynn and Vern used an extra-long level to accurately mark a grid for the slate tiles and to correct the angled line of the chimney.

Garden Wall ▲

An ordinary flat wall gains new dimension with a square of dark green painted on a field of lighter green. Strips of quick-release painter's tape help create the crisp edges of the square. The dark green area serves as a blank canvas on which Vern grouped clear glass vases designed to hang on the wall. Each holds water and a flower stem for simple elegance and color. The swing-arm lamp is one of two that Vern purchased to brighten the room at night.

Beauty and the Behemoth ▲

One of the homeowners bluntly described their gigantic 65-inch television as a "big black box." To let the fireplace take center stage in the living room, Vern relocated the existing entertainment center and the ultrahefty TV to the opposite wall. Originally, the storage piece lacked doors, so Amy Wynn cut bifold doors for the center portion, which hides the TV, and recessed doors for flanking cabinets that hold what Vern describes as "huge canoes of speakers." Painting the entire piece white unifies the new components with the old and gives the unit a fresh appearance.

Terrific Tile
On the floor, wall, or countertop, tiles can make your room more beautiful.

Visit any home center store, flooring specialist, or tile dealer, and you'll be amazed by the array of tiles available. Nearly endless colors, shapes, sizes, patterns, textures, and materials make it possible to create one-of-a-kind looks. On vertical and horizontal surfaces alike, tile is beautiful, durable, and easy to care for.

Mixing and matching tile sizes, shapes, and colors allows you to create original designs and establish a color palette for your room. Most tile dealers will help you plan a design using different tiles, such as a rug design fashioned entirely from various tile colors and shapes; or you can design a pattern on your own.

Glazed ceramic tiles are only one option. Tiles are also available in unglazed terra-cotta as well as in natural stone, including granite, limestone, marble, and slate. If those materials aren't in your budget, you can sometimes save money by choosing ceramic tiles that look like stone.

To bring more dimension to surfaces, embossed tiles feature images raised above the tile surface; hand-painted tiles can lend an artistic touch. Hand-thrown tiles offer a rustic look with their undulating surfaces. If you come across expensive tiles that you love, purchase a few to intersperse in a field of plain tiles.

Grout, the material used to fill in seams between tiles, comes in sanded and unsanded varieties and in numerous colors. On floors and countertops, you may be happier with darker grout tones, rather than white or off-white, because dirt won't show as much.

Tips for Installing Ceramic Tiles

In the world of do-it-yourself projects, anyone can learn to install tile. If you plan to tile a floor, consider purchasing pads designed to strap to your knees. Then follow these basics for beautiful results.

1 Find the center point of the room and draw a line through it from one end of the room to the other. Dry-lay tiles, leaving about ¼ inch between them. (Or use plastic spacers, available at home centers and flooring stores, to keep the distance between tiles consistent.) Shift tiles left or right to minimize the amount of cutting you'll need to do around the edges of the room. Mark where tiles should fall in this first row and pick up the tiles. Using a notched trowel (A), apply mastic formulated for tiles to a 3-foot section.

2 Lay the first tile in the adhesive, following the pencil marks. Use temporary spacers to keep grout lines even. Continue laying tiles (B) until you reach tiles that need to be cut. Cut remaining tiles with a tile cutter or a tile saw; for small cuts or shapes, use tile nippers. Let mastic dry according to manufacturer directions.

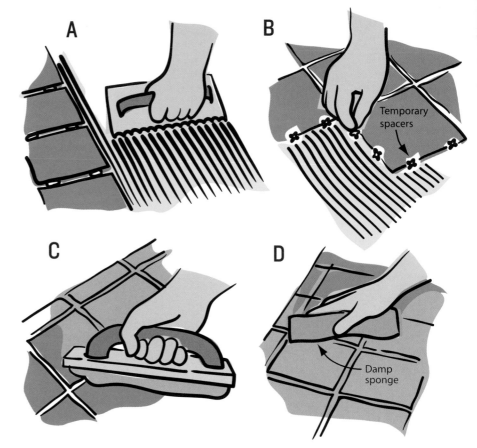

3 Remove the spacers. (Needlenose pliers can help with this step.) Use a float to apply grout (C). Allow grout to set as recommended by the manufacturer. Wipe away grout residue with a damp sponge (D). Rinse the sponge frequently to get tile faces as clean as possible. Allow grout to dry as recommended by the manufacturer.

Tile Nippers — Little bites make tiles fit tight.

Aptly named, this tool allows you to nip small bites out of tiles. Tile nippers are handy tools for tile installations. Use them to make straight or shaped cuts so that tiles fit in an irregular spot or snug around curved objects such as pipes. To cut more than 1 inch off the edge of a tile, use a tile cutter or tile saw. Then bite into the tile with the nippers to remove additional small curved or straight pieces. Purchase a pair designed to bite through the thickness of the tile you want to cut.

To make curved or straight irregular cuts, trace the outline of the cut you want to make onto paper; then transfer the outline onto the tile face. Carefully nip away the excess until you create the shape and size you need. Tile nippers can also shape glass or mirror pieces.

More Tile Style

The *Trading Spaces* designers often put the beauty of tile to work in their rooms. Take a look at this gallery of ideas using tile.

Think beyond store-bought ceramic. Apply tough, nonporous material as you would tile; then grout for a mosaiclike finished product. Consider using thrift store china, broken mirror pieces, glass beads, or shards of terra-cotta pots. Gen attached pieces of broken Fiestaware dishes behind the sink and then grouted the backsplash as if it were covered in tile.

Apply tile by the sheet. Look at home centers and flooring stores for vinyl and ceramic sheet goods featuring mini-tiles that are already connected into gridlike or mosaic patterns. The cost may be a bit more, but you'll save yourself hours of intricate installation work. In a Maine kitchen, Gen covered the existing countertop with preassembled sheets of small black and white tiles.

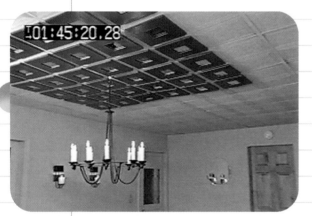

No tile? No problem! Great tiled looks don't require ceramic tile. Any flat, regular object can be applied in a gridlike pattern to a flat surface. Consider tiling walls, benches, tables, shelving, and more. For example, Vern tiled a Providence living room ceiling with 36 square mirrors.

Tile as a problem-solver. To fit standard tiles attractively onto some surfaces, you may need to cut down a few tiles with a wet saw or tile nippers. Or you can mix different sizes of the same tile pattern to get a tight fit. In Ft. Lauderdale: 59th Street, Frank broke two large tiles and placed bands of broken pieces between whole tiles.

Mix grout and glass. Treat glass fragments just like tiles: Attach the glass with a clear adhesive and then grout for a finished look. In California: Peralta Street, Hildi covered the fireplace in chips of glass and grout.

The homeowners want more color and style in their family room. They also ask Frank to create canine-friendly quarters.

Before

Make It Mediterranean

STYLE LESSON: Say "welcome" with a host of hues borrowed from the Mediterranean.
BACKGROUND: Think of all the red tile roofs on a hillside in Italy or Greece, and you'll understand the beginnings of this Mediterranean-style family room filled with earthy hues. Inspired by lands that embody hospitality, this look is an ideal choice for a space where you plan to gather for good times.

All Things Aegean ◀

Diamond-motif fabric with hints of Grecian style and a gallon of red clay-color paint distinguish Frank's Mediterranean-inspired family room. Limiting this rich paint color to the wall surrounding the white-painted mantel ensures that all eyes focus on the fireplace to appreciate the dramatic contrasts of light and dark. Using darker glaze, Frank painted faux cracks and softened the lines with a sponge, creating the illusion that this wall is well-aged and weathered—perfect for the Mediterranean theme. Dressing end walls in a lighter version of the clay hue keeps the look in balance. Adding dashes of both colors to the mantel facade is an easy way to call attention to the molding details. To keep spending in check, only the sofa cushions are covered in the new fabric, adding color and pattern with a touch of European style to these plain, off-white seating pieces.

Supporting Roles ▶

Shelves offer an opportunity to think differently. This Mediterranean beauty features a basic painted 1×12 as the shelf surface; two shapely black iron planter baskets stand in as clever shelf supports. Frank and Paige whipped up the sculpture, which features metal rebar and a wood block for the base.

Ancient and Classic ▼

This classic coffee table can serve up conversation as well as the coffee. Centered on a new rug in colors that complement the walls, the coffee table features four supports fashioned from plaster capitals. Painted black, the capitals match the black marble slab tabletop. No Mediterranean trip is complete without a glimpse of some ancient ruins: The angled and unpolished edge of the tabletop recalls images of the Parthenon and Acropolis.

85

The existing tile floor in this Texas family room feels comfortably cool during hot summers. Still, an area rug is a warm, welcome addition.

TOOLBOX Square and Level

Every home toolbox needs a carpenter's square and level. You'll find the square (or a tri-square) handy whenever you want to create perfect 90-degree angles—when you're building a basic cube (see page 148), constructing partition walls, or drawing a geometric pattern on a wall or other surface. A long level makes big jobs easier (such as drawing long horizontal or vertical lines on a wall or aligning multiples of an object for hanging on the wall); a torpedo level like the one pictured is useful for smaller jobs, such as making sure artwork is hanging straight or checking more diminutive pieces of custom-built furniture.

Doggie Toy Chest ▲

An unfinished chest, available at home centers and crafts stores, lets you try out fun faux techniques. Frank purchased this lidded beauty to stash toys for the homeowners' dogs. Dragging a combing tool through colored glaze creates the subtle strié pattern on the front. *To learn some faux-painting techniques, including combing, turn to page 42.*

Curtain Call ◄

A niche for a big-screen television beside the mantel makes this room multipurpose: The homeowners can watch the big game or chat by the fireside—or both. Soft green tab-top panels cover the nearby window to darken the room for tube time. Frank nabbed these treatments for less than $15 per panel—too good of a deal to pass up, even though the panels required shortening to fit.

Table for a Song ▲

Every home center has the makings for an end table like this one, and you won't have to spend a bundle for the materials. Look in the unfinished furniture section for tabletops, legs, braces, and other decorative touches in a style that suits your space. For the tabletop, rout the edges of a 20×20-inch piece of solid birch. For the base, purchase four turned legs and join with a framework of 1× pieces for support. Frank lightly washed the tabletop with transparent golden paint so the beauty of the wood shows through. For the legs he applied glaze that matches the walls.

..**87**

Concealed in Style ▶

A single bifold door stands in as a colorful screen to hide a telephone in one corner of the room. Clay-color paint topped with three bands of gold, brown, and green quickly transforms the door at minimal cost. Keep your own screen project simple like this one or try the more challenging design *below*.

Make Your Own Screen Gem

One basic wood frame and simple hardware are the beginnings of a screen that you can adapt to perfectly complement any style decor.

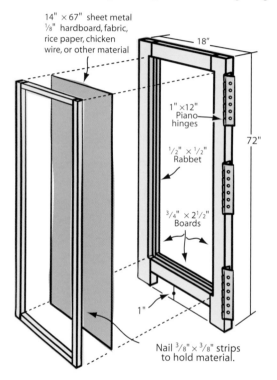

14" × 67" sheet metal ⅛" hardboard, fabric, rice paper, chicken wire, or other material

18"

1" ×12" Piano hinges

½" × ½" Rabbet

¾" × 2½" Boards

72"

1"

Nail ⅜" × ⅜" strips to hold material.

Build this basic wood frame or have someone construct it for you. Then choose how you want to finish the center panel. If you opt for ⅛-inch hardboard, you can prime and paint the piece as desired, perhaps using stencils or faux-finishing techniques. Or cover the panel with wallpaper or fabric over a layer or two of batting. Finish the back of the board attractively too.

For a more industrial look, sandwich a piece of sheet metal between the frames. Sheets of rice paper

allow you to create a shoji-like screen. Chicken wire can work in a country or contemporary setting, depending on how you finish the frame. For a country look, tuck a few dried flowers into the screen. Keep the wire unadorned for a sleek, modern design.

If building this frame isn't an option, join three 79×14¾-inch hollow-core bifold closet doors, using three bifold door hinges between panels. Then embellish panels with paint, fabric, wallcovering, sheet metal, buttons, ribbons, tassels, or braiding—or whatever appeals to you.

88 Freestanding screens are versatile: Use one to balance awkward architecture, to divide a room, or to hide an unattractive view.

Screens to Inspire

Whether you want to balance an awkward space, hide an unattractive view, or divide a space, a freestanding screen can provide the solution.

Fascinating fabric. Get the most bang for your buck by using free-hanging or framed swaths of fabric to screen off or divide a space. Laurie used a large piece of fabric in a wooden frame, suspended from the ceiling with chain, to separate the two functional areas in a living/dining room in Austin.

Screen door solution. Metal screening for screen doors is inexpensive, versatile, and available in several metallic finishes. Use wire cutters, tin snips, a staple gun, and heavy gloves to stretch the screen across the frame. Doug folded lengths of silver screening accordion-style and nailed the screening in a pass-through between the living room and the kitchen in Colorado.

Chain gang. As you create custom screening, remember those beaded dorm curtains. Nearly any stringlike material can be hung vertically and en masse for a screen effect. In a New Orleans basement office, Gen established a cozy seating area by hanging lengths of chain from the ceiling and attaching wood laminate rectangles in random places.

The height of fashion. To fit a screen into a space with an angled ceiling (attic rooms, understair storage areas), connect panels of various heights in a stair-step fashion to match the angle of the ceiling. In Austin: La Costa Drive, Ty installed various sizes of two-tone wooden louvered panels to follow the ceiling line and screen off a storage area.

Solid materials. When in doubt about which style of screen is right for a room, go with a classic wood or wood shutter screen. Solid screens offer versatility and effectively obscure unattractive views or furniture. In Colorado: Cherry Street, Laurie disguised the side of a large-screen TV from the room's entry with a traditional accordion screen painted to complement the room.

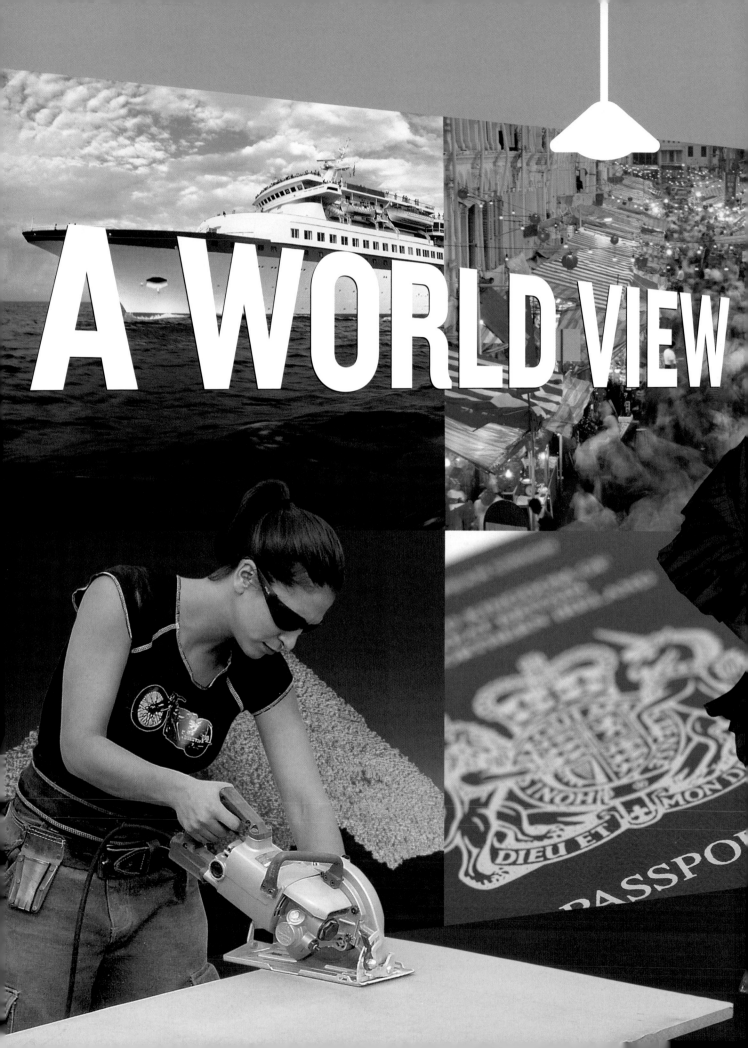

A WORLD VIEW

Chapter 5: A World View Planes, trains, ships, and automobiles—now it's easier than ever to travel and tote home treasures to remind you of the fun you had. Of course, plenty of stores have already done the importing for you. Turn the page to see how beautiful the trappings of another culture can be in your home.

Before

Pink isn't pretty anymore
for these homeowners.
They're ready to see the
white wicker go too.

South American Sex Appeal

STYLE LESSON: Balance masculine and feminine details with wood and fabric. **BACKGROUND:** Admittedly, this master bedroom was way too girlie for a young couple. So Gen equalizes the masculine and the feminine using an oh-so-sexy combination of rich brown leathers and luxurious red velvet.

Grand Gaucho Character ◀

Gen set out to infuse this master bedroom with both masculine and feminine elements to please a married couple. Inspired by the rough and rugged clothing, colors, and materials associated with Argentine gauchos—ranch hands as dear to the Argentine culture as the cowboy is to the States—Gen shaped a new look for the room that's as pleasing to a man as it is to a woman.

Soft, touchable leather and luxurious red velvet are important decorating components in this makeover. Rich brown paint on the walls establishes a sense of intimacy and warmth for the room while making a clear connection to the use of leather and the more masculine side of the theme. The red velvet brings its own brand of warmth to the room, but speaks to the more feminine side.

Gen decided on a headboard woven with two shades of leather at the top of the piece and finished with soft red velvet near the bottom, creating a dramatic focal point for the room. The velvet, she says, is "for their heads. This approach is so simple. You can do weaving with fabric, leather, soft woods, and even metals."

To learn the basics for weaving materials on walls and other surfaces, see page 76.

Extravagant Dashes ▼

Because the red velvet material cost a pricey $24 a yard and Gen could only afford 4 yards, she made wise use of leftover fabric from the headboard to fashion a few pillows and bolsters. Other pillows feature wide, casual flanges and striped fabrics in white and black.

To learn how to sew your own bolster-style pillow, turn to page 60.

Inspirational Stuff

Keep your eye out for the next great design idea. You may discover a look you love at work or at play—or perhaps you'll find it in the most unexpected locations.

Gen found her muse for this master bedroom in Argentine gauchos. Turn to the world around you for an unlimited supply of design ideas. Fabrics often play an important inspirational role in a room makeover. Study the motifs on dishware or the designs and colors on a rug or purchased pillows. Notice what elements in nature capture your fancy—a beautiful rock or the surface of a leaf perhaps. Visit the library and find books on eras that interest you. If you're fascinated by the 1940s, for example, look at magazines and books from that period to gain an understanding of the elements of design that were popular at the time.

Sealing the Connection ◄

Making the connection to the Argentine cowboys clear, Gen glued and sealed photographs of these cultural icons to the raised panels on brown-painted closet doors. At the foot of the bed, the bench features new leather upholstery and red velvet bolsters.

Image-Conscious ◄

Gen's purse served as a model for this saddle artwork done on a black gesso. Light brown accents give an aged appearance to the completed image. If you don't like to paint or draw freehand, use an opaque projector to cast an image on the surface; then trace or paint the outline.

TOOLBOX

Sewing Machine
Buy this useful tool, and you'll soon be in stitches.

Visit any store where sewing machines are sold, and you'll find many options to choose from. Most sewing machines work basically alike, but some models have more bells and whistles than others. If you plan to sew pillows and hems, then a machine that only sews straight stitches forward and backward may suit you fine. However, if you want to experiment with more detail and increasingly complex stitches, consider a fancy computer-driven model. Of course, the more capabilities your machine offers, the more you'll pay. You'll probably be happiest choosing the best you can afford. After you get your machine home, study the owner's manual and take a sewing class or two to explore the possibilities.

Design with Decoupage

This sticky business can beautify all kinds of surfaces.

Decoupage medium is a clear-drying glue, sealer, and finish all in one that lets you apply images to almost any surface and protect your work.

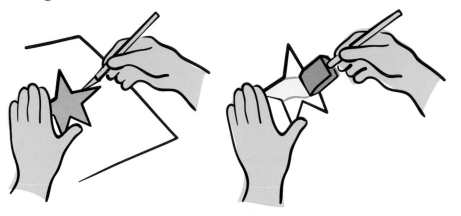

Crafts stores and online sources offer decoupage images you can cut out. Motifs run an almost unlimited gamut from fish to flowers and hot air balloons to historical documents. If you can't find decoupage paper you like, consider other heavier papers, such as wrapping paper or greeting cards. Or photocopy clipart images onto quality paper. Avoid using paper with printing on both sides of the page.

A Cut decoupage motifs or images from the paper with a small pair of very sharp scissors. Or use a crafts knife with a self-healing cutting mat underneath to protect the work surface.

B Using a disposable foam brush (or a paintbrush), apply decoupage medium to the back of each motif.

C Adhere image to the surface. (Surface should be painted or stained in advance, if needed, and clean.) If excess decoupage medium seeps from beneath the motifs, wipe it away with a damp sponge. After all motifs are in place, cover the entire surface with a thin, even layer of decoupage medium using a foam brush to seal. Ensure the motif edges are well-adhered to the surface. To prevent the surface from feeling tacky, coat the dry decoupage medium with clear acrylic sealer.

You can substitute any type of white glue—thinned with water—for decoupage medium. After applying glue to the back of the motif, press it to the surface and wipe with a damp sponge, working from the center to the edges to smooth out bubbles.

Fun with Photos

Personalize your spaces with photographs of family, friends, pets, or places and things you love. Mine photo albums and test out these ideas at your house.

Zoom and crop. Create large-scale copies of images at a copy center. Use a straightedge to trim the pictures in unusual ways. Don't be afraid to chop off part of the main subject in the image. In a living room, Gen cropped copies of family photos and then decoupaged the images to cabinet doors.

Embellish and illuminate. Photocopy favorite photos and then glue or decoupage the paper images to a lampshade. Experiment with different thicknesses and types of paper to get the transparent effect you desire. In New Jersey: Lafayette Street, Vern mounted pictures of the homeowners' baby on the shades of three wall sconces.

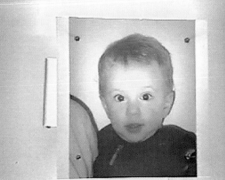

Iron on images. Purchase an iron-on transfer kit (available at crafts and computer stores) and use an ink-jet printer to create personalized transfers that you can apply to fabric. In Colorado, Gen printed pictures onto transfer paper and then ironed the images onto slipcovers for the dining chairs.

Enlarge and frame.
Who knew you could be a superstar so easily? Work with a photography supply store or frame shop to enlarge, dry-mount on poster board, and frame a personal photo—to stunning effect. In Houston: Sawdust Street, Doug blew up a sexy photo of a homeowner and hung the piece above a living room fireplace.

Collect and collage. Gather a host of images—from a specific event, of one person through the years, or another theme—and create a photo collage. Layer the images on foam-core or poster board and frame the collage. In a living room, Vern put together an "image quilt" that combined printed nature images and family photos in a geometric quilt design.

Style from the Nile

What could be more intriguing than the Land of Pyramids?

STYLE LESSON: Add sophistication with exotic features.
BACKGROUND: Kia decides to do an Egyptian theme in this master bedroom using ancient icons, jewel tones, and luxurious fabrics.

Fit for a King and Queen ▼

Ancient Egyptian rulers are known for having enjoyed riches beyond imagination. So it fits that Kia lavishes this ancient Egyptian-themed master bedroom with rich, sumptuous colors that she playfully dubs "Tut Wine" and "Pharaoh Gold." A gold-painted Eye of Horus, which according to Kia is a protective eye, serves as theme-appropriate artwork.

Of Pyramids and Palms ◄

No Egyptian-theme space is complete without a few pyramids, and Kia obliges with several—a pyramid-shape pillow on the bed and wood cornices featuring pyramid-shape cutouts at the center. Covered with batting and fabric, the cornices have a soft, opulent look that suits the setting. The cornices also serve the practical purpose of hiding the rod used to hang the curtain panels. Appropriately, silk palm fronds were attached to fan blades overhead. To finish the room, Kia playfully left a hieroglyphic message for the homeowners on the freestanding screen in the corner. It reads, "David loves Noel."

Crown the Bed ▲

Elegantly dressed in green velvet and fitted with golden monolith posts, a once-ordinary headboard brings sculptural beauty into the bedroom. There's another lesson here: Don't pass up expensive fabrics that you truly love. Kia found incredible fabric with an Egyptian motif for $69 a yard. Rather than let it go, she bought what she could afford and employed it as a dramatic backdrop.

Before

The homeowners find the spotty furnishings and orange and cream walls uninspiring. They request dark, warm colors and an atmosphere for romance.

Soft-Touch Cornice

Top windows with stylish fabric-wrapped structures.

An upholstered cornice gives you two design bonuses: pleasing architecture and soft, textural fabric over cushiony batting. Decorative cording, braid, tassels, buttons, or other embellishments can make your creation one-of-a-kind.

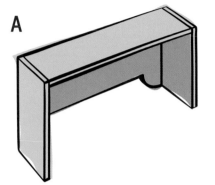

A

B

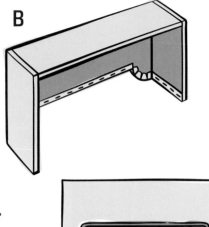

C

D

A Make a boxlike cornice out of ½- or ¾-inch plywood, following the basics for building a wooden cube on page 148. For extra embellishment, shape the bottom edge of the cornice as desired using a paper pattern and a jigsaw.

B Cut a piece of batting slightly larger than the front and sides of the cornice box. Spray front, sides, and top of box with spray adhesive. Wrap batting around surfaces; press firmly to adhere. Trim excess. Lay fabric on surface wrong side up and position cornice facedown on fabric. Cut and trim fabric, allowing enough fabric to wrap to back of cornice. Staple to secure.

C Cut piece of fabric to fit inside back and returns of the cornice. Secure with spray adhesive.

D Hot-glue decorative cording or other embellishments to front and sides of cornice.

Circular Saw **Make quick work of cutting wood.**

Valued for its portability and ability to rip or crosscut lumber and sheet goods, a circular saw is a good investment for your home tool kit. This handy power tool can also make bevel and miter cuts without a lot of effort. For most do-it-yourself jobs, purchase a 1-hp model with a 7¼-inch blade. If you prefer a cordless version, you may be limited to a 6- or 6½-inch model. Purchase a combination blade, which will rip and crosscut, and also buy a plywood blade, which features numerous closely spaced teeth for smooth cuts. Always wear safety goggles when using a power saw of any kind.

Wow Windows

If windows offer a glimpse into the soul of your house, then the window treatments should tell something about your spirited approach to decorating.

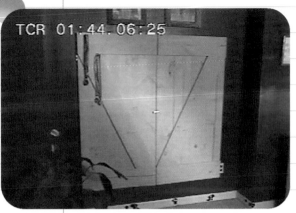

Shutter at the thought. Look for premade shutters at home centers, buy vintage shutters from flea markets, or attach trimmed architectural details in the manner of shutters. In Orlando: Winterhaven, Doug hung two barn doors around a window in place of traditional shutters.

Go totally faux. In windowless rooms or rooms with poorly placed windows, build a window frame with door molding and hang it on the wall. For a more natural look, add a sill and grille to the frame. In a San Diego kitchen, Laurie fashioned a faux window by attaching a wood frame to the wall and then dressing it like a real window.

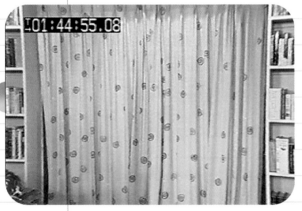

Stamp on some style. Combine stencils or stamps and acrylic paint to enliven neutral window treatments. Remove the treatments, lay fabric flat, and embellish. In a library/living room in Boston, Frank saved money and time by stamping existing draperies with a foam stamp and red fabric paint.

Clip on the trimmings. For maximum versatility, choose simple window treatments such as cafe curtains and basic panels that hang from metal clips. Or develop your own flexible window treatment hardware with clothespins, alligator clips, large-scale paper clips, and other adjustable fasteners. In a Seattle living room, Frank attached colorful place mats to a simple valance using custom-painted clothespins.

Color a canvas. Think of a closed blind as a blank canvas for you to paint, stain, stencil, and embellish. Apply different complementary designs or colors to each side of the blind for extra interest. In Austin: Wyoming Valley Drive, Hildi quickly customized the existing wooden blinds in a kitchen by giving them a blended coat of black and orange paint.

Chapter 6: Charmed They're Sure Some things are inherently charming and give you a little lift—like a quaint bed and breakfast, children's games, and afternoon tea. Wouldn't life be more fun if you surround yourself with the things that delight you? Watch for the "special somethings" in the rooms that follow.

CHARMED
THEY'RE SURE

103

Country Cleans Up

STYLE LESSON: Metal and paint refresh a country look in a kitchen.
BACKGROUND: Gen erases outdated elements and successfully uses a tin ceiling and sage-green chalkboard paint on the walls to put a playful yet contemporary spin on country.

Clever Cover-Ups ◄

Cute country has had its day, but Gen's design gives the homeowners a clean, contemporized version of country style. An overabundance of natural wood tones, including the floor, cabinetry, and dining tabletop, left the kitchen looking a little bland. On the soffit above the cabinets, a hand-stenciled country-style border was passé.

Paint and an embossed tin ceiling provide the visual relief that Gen envisions and serve as the foundation for the theme: a French *boucherie,* or butcher shop.

Artistic Turns ◄

Paint the color of French vanilla gives the cabinetry a buttery glow, offering a pleasant departure from natural wood without sacrificing warmth. New brushed-chrome knobs update the cabinetry, and their simple style balances the more ornate design of the silvery metal ceiling. Soft gray paint emphasizes the traditional recessed panels on all the cabinet doors and makes another visual connection to the ceiling material.

For fun on the backsplashes and as a reference to the butcher shop theme, Gen and the neighbors hang framed photographs they took of "meat puppets"—caricatures they fashioned using meat and produce from the supermarket.

Before 7.15.2

Though the homeowners adore the wood floor, they're more than willing to eliminate cutesy country features, such as a busy stenciled border, and break up the abundance of wood by doing something different with the cabinets.

Chalk Up Some Style ▲

Continuing the French butcher shop theme, sage green chalkboard paint lends practicality and beauty to the walls. Applied over a coat of tinted primer, the chalkboard paint (available in black and green colors at home centers and crafts stores) dries into a surface that you can write on with chalk. The smooth painted finish wipes clean with a chalkboard eraser or a soft, damp cloth.

Tin Ceiling Basics

Hide an unattractive ceiling and boost beauty.

Plan to have a helper assist you with this project and allow two weekends for completion. You'll find that the appealing results are worth the effort.

Tin or embossed metal ceiling panels typically measure 2×8 feet or 2×4 feet. Manufacturers usually provide installation instructions. Most suggest either nailing the panels to furring strips that are secured to the ceiling joists or covering the entire ceiling with ⅜-inch plywood panels secured to ceiling joists. Using a layer of plywood is considered the quicker method.

After the plywood is in place, find the center of the ceiling and snap a chalk line down the middle. Use the line as a guide for aligning the panels because most rooms aren't perfectly square.

Keep in mind that all metal ceilings tarnish. Most manufacturers recommend painting the metal with oil-base metallic paint or sealing the surface with clear polyurethane.

Drop ceiling tiles and embossed wallpaper that look like tin are also available. When using wallpaper, finish this treatment by applying silver metallic paint; then rub black paint on and off for the illusion of age.

REC   PAIGE CAM

Fun with Chalkboard Paint

Use this playful paint to cover a large expanse or a small area.

Imagine a space where it's OK to write on the walls. Chalkboard paints transform practically any surface into a note- or sketchbook where you can write and draw with chalk.

Chalkboard paint comes in black and green, and chalkboard spray paint is also available. You can paint one or more walls with chalkboard paint or you can paint only a portion of a wall with chalkboard paint and add borders of regular latex paint color, as on this backsplash (A).

When painting a small area, measure and mark a square, rectangle, or wide chair-rail-height border with a straightedge and pencil, and tape off the outline with painter's tape. After painting with tinted primer, let dry. Then roll or brush on the chalkboard paint; let dry to a smooth finish that you can write on with chalk.

If desired, paint or build a frame around your chalkboard to finish (B).

Chalkboard paint is a fun finish for furniture too, such as a wood toy chest or for drawer and door fronts (C).

Wipe off chalk with a chalkboard eraser (D) or rub gently with a cloth with warm water and mild detergent.

Always begin chalkboard paint projects with tinted primer and allow to dry before applying two or more coats of chalkboard paint.

Chalk Line

Get snappy with this handy tool.

To make a long, straight mark on a wall, ceiling, floor, or other large surface, such as a piece of plywood, use a chalk line. This nifty device features a metal casing with cording that winds around a bobbin inside the casing. Also inside is colored, powdered chalk, which adheres to the cord. To use the chalk line, make two or more marks on the surface to indicate where the line should begin and end. As you pull the cord from the metal casing, have a helper assist you in stretching the cord as tightly as possible, perfectly aligning it over the marks. With the cord tight, pull the cord away from the surface and let it go. The cord snaps back to the surface, leaving the powdered chalk in a perfect line between the marks—thus the term "snapping a chalk line."

Ceiling Chic

Consider the ceiling the fifth wall. After all, these *Trading Spaces* ceilings are worth looking up to!

Soften with fabric. Fabric-covered ceilings can be chic and refined or light and fanciful. Stretch fabrics tautly and finish with trim for a crisp look. Let sheer fabrics billow for a dreamy vista. Gen worked with an existing drop ceiling in a basement by weaving strips of white fabric across the drop ceiling supports.

Boost the style with beams. Make a high-ceilinged room more intimate or add interest to overwhelming space by outlining architectural features with wood trim crafted from 1×3s or 1×4s. In Texas, Doug accentuated the high ceiling in a playroom by attaching wooden beams in a simple barnlike formation.

Make your own drama. Any finish you apply to walls or furniture has potential as a ceiling finish. Consider adding stamping, stenciling, rag rolling, and other faux-painting techniques to your overhead world. In a bedroom, Frank painted a tray ceiling dark purple and then handpainted stars and other celestial bodies.

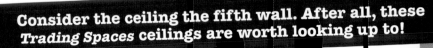

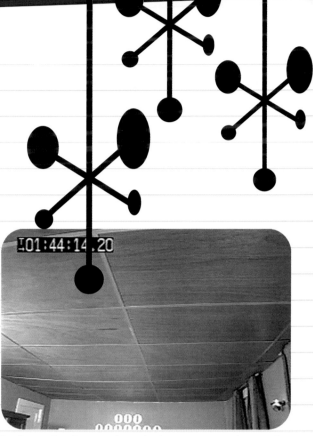

Drop in some class. Upgrade a drop ceiling by painting support beams and replacing foam tiles with wood, wire mesh, or new drop ceiling tiles (available through drop ceiling manufacturers) that mimic tin and other metals. In a living room in Providence: Phillips Street, Hildi improved a drop ceiling by replacing foam tiles with lightly stained sheets of lauan and painting the supports silver.

Soften with coving. Round off where walls and ceiling meet with coving. Look for molding that mimics rounded coving. In Maryland, Doug and Amy Wynn took room rounding to the extreme by attaching several L-shape supports to the walls and ceiling. They then bent strips of flexible hardboard and nailed them to the supports to create the curved effect of being inside a train car.

Tradition with a Twist
Laurie gives a fresh spin to the classics.

STYLE LESSON: Small surprises blow the dust off traditional style.
BACKGROUND: In this bedroom, Laurie sticks with the classics but updates the look with more-intense tones and unexpected furnishings.

Spice of Life ◀

Returning to her home turf of Jackson, Mississippi, Laurie combines fun with traditional style in a master bedroom. "We are going to bring some spice into this room," Laurie says. Keeping her promise, she finds fabric striped in tones of deep purple-red and rich gold and labels the colors eggplant and cumin. Gold walls set off the striped fabric, which upholsters a substantial 8-foot-tall headboard detailed with decorative nailhead trim. "It's amazing what a little nailhead trim will do," Laurie says. "It gives it a little bit of sparkle."

Southern Lightning ▶

Amy Wynn builds a chaise longue that the homeowner can use for relaxing and reading in front of the French doors "because every Southern woman needs a chaise longue," Laurie says. But this isn't the familiar "fainting couch" design. Instead, this clean-lined version zigzags like lightning on simple U-shape legs. For coordinating comfort, the chaise features a thick cushion covered in fabric reminiscent of a leopard print. A red pillow adds spicy color.

To keep the background tone-on-tone, draperies match the walls. Because Amy Wynn used only $66 of her $200 budget to purchase wood for the chaise, Laurie invested the remainder in attractive drapery rods, including swing-arm versions that allow floor-to-ceiling panels at the French doors to swing out of the way.

Before

TCR 01:43.03:14
V---- A----

After divorcing, the homeowner of this bedroom is ready for a new beginning. "It has lots of ghosts," she says. "Smash the furniture. I don't want to recognize anything!"

Let Color Flow ▲

Laurie devised strategies to keep the look restful for this bedroom. Deep eggplant paint visually lowers the high ceiling for more intimacy. Soffits forming the sides of the tray ceiling are painted to match the gold walls. "If we would have left the soffit white," Laurie says, "it chops up the room." Even the abstract artwork, painted by the neighbors, is done in tones similar to the wall color.

Get the Message ◄

In keeping with the tone-on-tone scheme, the drapery fabric repeats on upholstered boards flanking the armoire. Gold ribbon running diagonally around the boards fits snugly to hold photographs, messages, and other small items. To make a message board, cut plywood to the desired size. Wrap the board with batting, stapling the edges of the batting to the back of the plywood. Cover with fabric, stapling the fabric edges to the back of the plywood. Add ribbon.

> **When you see the dramatic fabric on the headboard,"** Laurie says, "the gold wall color is the perfect backdrop."

Ribbon Rendezvous ▲

Ribbon makes another special appearance in the bedroom—this time in a rainbow of colors. Wanting to dress up some chairs that belonged to the homeowner's grandmother, Laurie avoids the permanence of paint and opts instead to weave grosgrain ribbons through the spindles. Tiny dabs of hot glue hold the ends of the ribbons in place, making them easily removable if the homeowner tires of the look or wants to change ribbon colors.

Style from the Aisles ▲

Walk the aisles at any home improvement store, and you're sure to hit on creative ways to use ordinary items. These towel bars, which match the drapery rods in the room, are ideal for organizing reading material. When hanging rods such as these, be sure to use the appropriate hollow-wall anchor to keep them secure.

Amber Classic ▲

Keeping with *Trading Spaces* tradition, the ceiling fan came down to make way for a more stylish fixture. Laurie found this artsy amber light with a grape motif at a flea market. *To learn how to replace an existing ceiling fixture with a different fixture (new or old), turn to page 142.*

The color palette you choose for a room communicates mood. Autumnal colors, for example, make this bedroom warm and cozy—especially wonderful for colder months. To change the look for spring, a slipcover for the headboard and a duvet for the comforter could feature lighter, more airy hues, such as pale blues and yellows.

Decorative Nailhead Trim — Think of these details as "tacky" character you'll love.

Check hardware stores and home centers for these classic decorative details.

One *Trading Spaces* way to dress up upholstered pieces is to add decorative nailhead trim where fabric meets wood. Decorative nailheads come in many designs, from plain to ornate. Material options include brass and nickel and finishes such as antique, lacquered, burnished, and shiny. Decorative nailheads are available individually; they must be hammered in one by one. An accessory called a nail spacer can help you space nailheads neatly and evenly along the fabric edge. Or buy a continuous nail strip that looks like many nailheads joined together; with these you only drive a nailhead in every third, fourth, or fifth nail. Whether you're installing individual decorative nailheads or nailhead strips, use a lightweight tack hammer equipped with a nylon tip to avoid scuffing the decorative portion of the nail. To more easily remove decorative nails that are damaged or driven incorrectly, use a special tool called a tack lifter.

115

Upholster a Headboard

Get ready for a soft landing with these easy instructions.

The master bedroom is often the last place in the house to be decorated, but including a stylish upholstered headboard in your makeover plans will ensure that the finished design doesn't look like an afterthought.

To make an upholstered headboard, cut ½-inch plywood to the desired shape and size. Center and stretch two layers of acrylic batting over the plywood, wrapping a few inches of the batting around the edges to the back of the plywood and securing with spray adhesive and staples. (For extra cushion, first apply to the plywood a 1-inch piece of foam, cut to fit; secure with spray adhesive. Then cover the foam and plywood with batting as noted.)

Place decorator fabric right side down on a flat surface. Center the headboard, padded side down, on the fabric. Working on one side and then the other to create a smooth fit, pull the fabric over batting and staple to the back of the wood. Repeat pulling, wrapping, and stapling fabric on the bottom and top. Cut notches in fabric, if necessary, and neatly fold to fit into curves or around corners. Fold under and staple raw edges to hide them.

If desired, you can also add covered buttons to your headboard to create a tufted look. After covering buttons, mark locations where you want to place them. (Use a carpenter's level for this step so that buttons

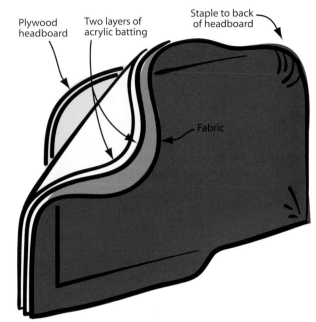

Plywood headboard

Two layers of acrylic batting

Staple to back of headboard

Fabric

remain in straight rows.) At each mark, place two staples in an X. Use a glue gun to secure one covered button over each pair of staples. You can customize your headboard further by gluing on decorative cording, braiding, or tassels.

To learn the simple steps for covering buttons, *turn to page 121.*

When choosing fabric to cover a headboard, select tighter weaves that won't overstretch and sag during high humidity. To ensure the best results with some patterns, such as stripes, take care that the motif is straight, level, and plumb.

TOOLBOX

Staple Guns and Nailers

When stapling and nailing, the *Trading Spaces* crew uses a compressor-driven nailer and stapler. You can buy more affordable electric versions and make quick work of your projects too. For an electric stapler suitable for upholstery and other lightweight jobs (staples about ³⁄₁₆-inch wide), expect to pay about $135. A 10-amp model electric nailer costs about $50 and fastens ⅝- to 1-inch brads—suitable for most do-it-yourself jobs. For both tools, purchase nails and staples designed for electric tools.

Happenin' Headboards

One of the most effective ways to give your bedroom a fresh look is to add a headboard. Let these *Trading Spaces* strategies inspire your own original design.

Think like a curtain maker. Many window treatments translate well to the wall behind the bed. Look for inspiring window treatments that feature dramatic hardware, rich fabrics, and architectural influences. Laurie attached a cornice board to the wall behind a bed and hung draperies from it, pulling the fabric down the wall and across the back of the bed.

Extend a theme. Whatever theme you choose for a bedroom, think of ways to extend it to the bed and headboard. In a boy's bedroom in Orlando: Winterhaven, Doug used holly tree limbs to extend his rustic theme: Larger logs served as main posts, and smaller, more flexible limbs curved across the back.

Oversize for multifunction and drama. Space permitting, allow an entire wall unit to serve as your headboard and the focal point of the bedroom. Combine wood, fabric, padding, shelving—even lighting—to fashion one multipurpose piece of furniture. Vern wove wide strips of two different iridescent fabrics to create a focal wall and padded headboard in California: Grenadine Way.

Take a cue from the architecture. Pay attention to ceiling line, angle, and pitch. High ceilings may require tall headboards; angular rooflines may suggests strongly geometric looks for the bed. In Plano: Shady Valley Road, Hildi built head- and footboards to match the steeply pitched cathedral ceiling.

Add exotic accents. Embellish a headboard that you already like by applying decorative wood trim, fabric, plant material, cloth fringe, and more. In this "Jungle Boogie" bedroom in Pennsylvania, Doug entirely covered an existing headboard with two sizes and colors of bamboo.

"It's too simple and flat," say the homeowners of the builder's-
grade fireplace in their new home. They're ready for some
distinctive style, and Doug's the guy to give it to them.

News Flash: Fireplace in Disguise!

STYLE LESSON: You can transform a plain fireplace.
BACKGROUND: Practically all the neighbors have the same fireplace, but Doug devises a clever cover-up that pairs nicely with an existing armoire. Newspaper motifs toss in a little fun.

Spanish Beauty ◄

The Spanish-style rustic pine armoire in this family room was definitely a keeper; Doug uses the armoire as a building block for the rest of the room makeover and designs a fireplace surround to match—complete with arched top and black iron elements. Smoky green walls set off the mixture of light and dark tones in the distressed pine pieces. The wall color also unites other furnishings that the homeowner already has on hand. Leaving the ceiling white prevents the room from appearing too dark.

Fireplace Finesse ►

Pine construction, an arched top, and "recessed panels" fashioned from moldings give the new fireplace surround a look very similar to the armoire. Even the black wrought-iron sconces are a visual reference to the hardware on the armoire. Doug experimented with various stain techniques until he found a match.

Newsworthy Seating ▼

Who knew you could land something so stylish at a consignment shop? That's where Doug found this funky armchair—covered in fabric that looks like layers of newspaper—for only $200. "Every room has to have a little quirk," he says.

When matching stain to an existing piece of furniture, test the stain color first on a scrap piece of the same lumber you plan to stain.

Room for Family ▲

Because the homeowners have three kids, they need plenty of comfortable seating. Doug arranges the leather sofa with a pair of chairs around a coffee table and anchors the grouping with a large area rug that complements the walls. Giant pillows—visible beyond the sofa—are great for lying on the floor in front of the fireplace or television.

More Good News! ▲

Always on the lookout for off-the-cuff artwork ideas, Doug covers a canvas stretched on a frame with random layers of current newspapers—all good news, of course—using a mixture of half white glue, half water.

Soft Touch ▲

A fabric-covered cornice lends a soft finished touch, mounted on the wall above the window treatments. You can also use a cornice to cover up plain curtain rods or to create the illusion of a taller window. *To learn how to make and cover a wooden cornice, turn to page 100.*

You can glue (or decoupage) other images, such as photographs or simple fabric motifs, onto canvas.

TOOLBOX

Self-Covered Button Kits

Dressing up a plain pillow can be as simple as adding a covered button to the middle. Fabric and crafts stores carry self-covered button kits for under $1. Buttons come in a number of sizes, but the larger sizes (1- or 2-inch) are often easier to cover and show up nicely on a wall or pillow. Look for assortments of fabric scraps at fabric and crafts stores. To cover a button, cut a circle of fabric ⅝ inch larger than the button form. Baste around the circle using large stitches and leaving long tails. Fold the fabric over the base, tightly gathering the threads and securing them with a knot. Position the button back on the fabric-covered half and press firmly to join.

Fireplace Cover-Up

Everything you need to make over your fireplace is at the home center.

Moldings teamed with 1× lumber provide the fodder for fixing up a plain fireplace. Study the illustrations to learn the basics of designing, assembling, and installing a new surround.

Transforming the look of a plain fireplace can begin with a trip to the molding aisle of the local home center. Once there, experiment with fireplace design ideas by layering various wood features, such as crown and half-round moldings, rosettes, plinth blocks, and ornate wood onlays, onto 1× boards. Create the illusion of recessed panels, for example, by cutting and mitering half-round

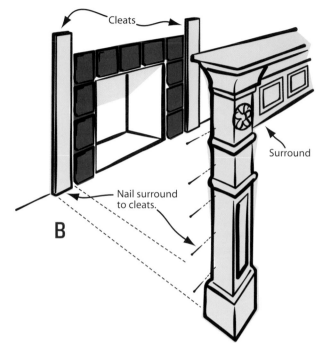

Cleats

Surround

Nail surround to cleats.

B

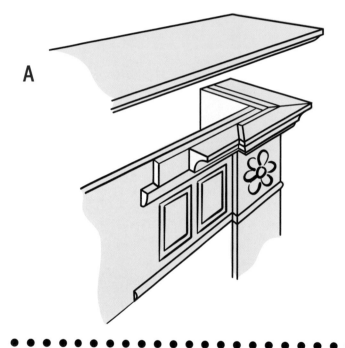

A

moldings to form rectangular or square "frames." Add detail beneath the mantel by using crown molding attached to a 1×3; add a piece of quarter round at the bottom edge of the 1×3 for a finished look (A). Finish-nail the various molding pieces to the 1× surround, countersink the nailhead, and fill the hole with wood putty before staining or painting. Attach the fireplace surround securely to the wall around the firebox, as shown (B).

Check architectural salvage stores, antiques stores, and flea markets for fireplace surrounds rescued from old houses. In areas of the country where old houses are more abundant, these cover-ups are still affordable.

Fast Fix-Ups

There's more than one way to transform a fireplace.

Installing a new surround isn't the only strategy for changing the look of your fireplace. Consider adding moldings above the mantel to the ceiling to emphasize vertical lines and give the fireplace a more substantial look. For more color, paint the mantel; or replace whole tiles around the firebox opening and on the hearth with a mosaic of brightly colored broken tiles, pieces of dishware, marbles, small mirrors, and other dimensional objects.

Distressed Looks for Furniture

Is it old or is it new? Here are some ways to quickly age just about any surface.

Use candle wax. For an aged look, use an old painter's trick: Thoroughly clean a finished or unfinished piece of furniture; then rub a wax candle over the piece wherever you'd like a distressed look. When you apply another coat of paint, the paint won't stick anywhere there's candle wax. In a Cincinnati living room, Frank aged a bench-shape coffee table using a similar technique.

Sand the surface. Sand a painted surface to remove layers of finish and reveal older layers or the original wood. Sandpaper works well on small projects, but consider an electric sander for larger pieces. Gen distressed the woodwork in a New Orleans bedroom by randomly applying a sander.

Attack the surface! Speed up the aging process by using sharp, heavy metal tools to introduce years of wear. Use hammers, chisels, old screwdrivers, and other (preferably old) tools. Always wear safety goggles. In an Oregon kitchen, Frank and his team distressed a tabletop by banging the wood with hammers and other random metal tools.

Get rough. To create exceptionally hard-worn surfaces, use anything that will tear up the piece—beat it with a heavier object, leave it in the rain, or toss it from a high height. In New Jersey, Doug built large candleholders that he and Ty distressed by using them as swords in a sword fight.

Paint and then sand. Apply a coat of paint to an unfinished or finished surface. Wait for the paint to dry and then sand the freshly painted surface, revealing the paint or wood tone below. In New Jersey: Manitoba Trail, Frank painted the living/dining room wood floor green and then distressed it with an orbital sander.

Chapter 7 : It's Like This... You never know what might turn on your decorating lightbulb and inspire a room transformation. Imitation may be the sincerest form of flattery—but it's also a smart way to build a look for your rooms. Take a look at how the *Trading Spaces* crew sometimes shapes a room using one thing as inspiration. You'll be inspired too!

Beauty by the Box

STYLE LESSON: Simple items can prompt elegance.
BACKGROUND: Inspired by the familiar blue box from Tiffany & Co., Hildi wraps this room in aqua. Meandering ribbons of airbrushed white are reminiscent of the ribbons around the famous box.

Simple Elegance ◄

Making the most of a small bedroom, Hildi transforms it into a blue oasis. The trademark blue box associated with Tiffany & Co. serves as her muse. After removing the chair rail "to enhance the size of the room," Hildi says, she chooses the signature aqua blue for all the walls. A duvet and shams perfectly match the pale blue hue. As a nod to the luxurious white ribbon around every box from the famous jeweler, Hildi directs the neighbor to airbrush free-form ribbons of white on the walls as well as on the duvet and shams. "You have to tap into your creative nature and free spirit," Hildi says. "The graffiti is very loose. It's simple and elegant."

Acrylic Aglow ◄

Hildi asks Ty to build lighted acrylic nightstands that merge traditional and modern styles. Hildi then tops both tables with polished silver pieces for classic elegance.

Before

The homeowners love their old colonial-style house, but they want a new look for the bedroom. One homeowner loves pastel blue, and she's hoping for a look that's light and airy.

If free-flowing designs don't appeal to you, use stencils or stamps. Or use an opaque projector to project an image from a photograph, book, magazine, or fabric onto the wall. Trace the outline and paint.

Shades of Style ▲

Roman shades match the bedding—right down to the airbrushed ribbons of white. The soft colors of the walls and fabric allow the existing mahogany furniture to stand out and add richness to the room. *To learn how to make your own Roman shades, turn to page 130.*

To learn how to make your own Roman shades, turn to page 130.

Artistic Endings ▲

A canvas washed in shades of aqua blue and brown repeats color from the walls and wood furniture. To bring more silver to this side of the room, Hildi flanks the painting with silver candle sconces. Below it, the wood bench is covered in pieces of tinfoil adhered shiny side up to the bench surface with spray adhesive. Look for silver items, such as old-fashioned "loving cups," at bargain prices at flea markets.

128

Spray Paint

For smooth finishes and quick makeovers, few techniques can top spray-painting.

TOOLBOX

Though a professional might use an airbrush or an airless paint sprayer, you can get professional results with an ordinary can of spray paint.

Perform quick transformations and keep your budget in check by using can spray paint. Hardware stores, home centers, and paint and crafts stores are all usually well-stocked with spray paints in a wide range of colors, sheens, and metallic tones. Newer formulas even simulate stone, metal, and fabric surfaces. The secret behind professional results is to keep your arm moving as you spray, and apply only a thin layer of paint at a time to avoid drips; don't hold the can nozzle too close to the surface you're painting. Also, begin spraying just off the surface of the piece and end spraying off the opposite side of the piece. Shake the can for as long as the manufacturer suggests and always experiment on a scrap piece of lumber or poster board before spray-painting the real project. Work in a well-ventilated room (or outdoors, whenever possible) and wear safety goggles and a dust mask (or a respirator-type mask when indoors).

Worried that their friends won't like the Tiffany-themed treatment, the neighbors write a conciliatory note on the wall. As it turns out, their concerns are unfounded. The homeowners love the look.

Dude, They made me do it! - Sean

29

Make a Roman Shade

Basic sewing skills are all you need to make one of these window treatments.

Raised, this treatment offers lavish folds of fabric. Lowered, the pattern and color become part of the decor. Like pillows, a shade can dress up or down, depending on the details.

● ●

1 **To determine shade length,** measure window length inside window frame; add 5½ inches. To determine shade width, measure window width inside window frame; add 1 inch. Using these measurements, cut same-size pieces to serve as a front and back for the shade.

2 **With right sides facing,** use ½-inch seam allowances to sew front and back together along sides and bottom. Turn right side out; press. Baste upper edges together.

3 **Place shade facedown on a flat surface.** Mark a horizontal line 5 inches from top edge. Mark three vertical lines, one centered and one 4 inches from each side edge. Beginning 8 inches from bottom edge, evenly mark ring placement 8 to 12 inches apart along vertical lines, aligning the markings horizontally. Tack ½-inch diameter plastic rings in place, sewing through both fabric layers.

4 **Cut 1×2 mounting board** 1 inch shorter than the shade width. Wrap top 5 inches of shade around board, aligning the marked horizontal line on the shade with top front edge of board; staple shade to board.

5 **Install a screw eye on underside of board** above each row of rings. Decide whether the draw cord will be on the left or right side of the shade; install a screw eye 1 inch from that end of the mounting board.

6 **Cut a ½-inch-diameter dowel** 2 inches shorter than shade width. Using a seam ripper, make a small opening in one side seam right above the bottom row of rings. Slip dowel into the opening; sew closed.

7 **Place shade facedown on a flat surface.** Cut a length of cord long enough to thread through a row of rings and the screw eyes and hang halfway down the shade. Tie one end of cord to a bottom ring. Thread cord through rings from bottom to top, then through screw

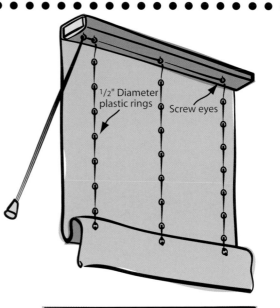

½" Diameter plastic rings   Screw eyes

eyes to the pull side of the shade. Thread remaining rows of rings in same manner.

8 **Mount shade inside window frame with screws.** With the shade lowered, adjust cords so shade is level and knot cords together outside the last screw eye. Cut cord ends to desired length and braid, if desired. Insert ends of cords through drapery pull; knot ends. Install awning cleat on pull side of window frame at desired height.

● ●

If sewing isn't your strength, look for basic Roman shades in neutral fabrics at discount or department stores. Use iron-on transfers, fabric pens, stencils, stamps, or embroidery ribbon to add custom touches.

Make It Yours: Side Tables

Before painting one of these side tables, sand off the glossy finish and remove the drawers. Then personalize the piece with paint and other materials to make it yours!

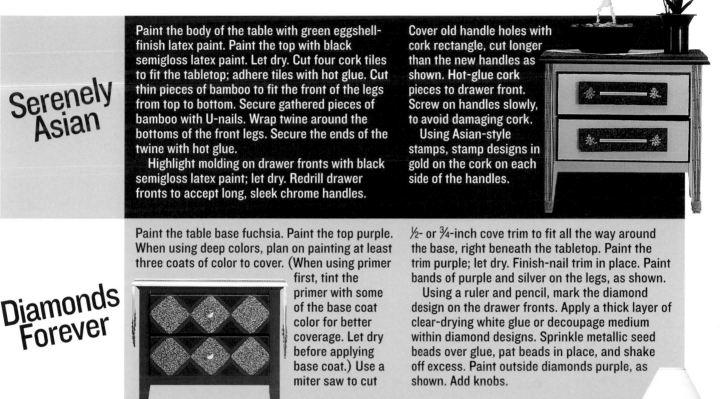

Serenely Asian

Paint the body of the table with green eggshell-finish latex paint. Paint the top with black semigloss latex paint. Let dry. Cut four cork tiles to fit the tabletop; adhere tiles with hot glue. Cut thin pieces of bamboo to fit the front of the legs from top to bottom. Secure gathered pieces of bamboo with U-nails. Wrap twine around the bottoms of the front legs. Secure the ends of the twine with hot glue.

Highlight molding on drawer fronts with black semigloss latex paint; let dry. Redrill drawer fronts to accept long, sleek chrome handles.

Cover old handle holes with cork rectangle, cut longer than the new handles as shown. Hot-glue cork pieces to drawer front. Screw on handles slowly, to avoid damaging cork.

Using Asian-style stamps, stamp designs in gold on the cork on each side of the handles.

Diamonds Forever

Paint the table base fuchsia. Paint the top purple. When using deep colors, plan on painting at least three coats of color to cover. (When using primer first, tint the primer with some of the base coat color for better coverage. Let dry before applying base coat.) Use a miter saw to cut

½- or ¾-inch cove trim to fit all the way around the base, right beneath the tabletop. Paint the trim purple; let dry. Finish-nail trim in place. Paint bands of purple and silver on the legs, as shown.

Using a ruler and pencil, mark the diamond design on the drawer fronts. Apply a thick layer of clear-drying white glue or decoupage medium within diamond designs. Sprinkle metallic seed beads over glue, pat beads in place, and shake off excess. Paint outside diamonds purple, as shown. Add knobs.

Playtime

Mask off outer edge of drawer fronts using painter's tape. Paint drawer fronts red. Always remove tape before paint dries; let dry. Tape around red drawer fronts, exposing primed edges. Paint primed areas white; let dry. Paint knobs blue; let dry. Attach to drawers.

Paint base yellow; let dry. Using a ruler and pencil, draw a checkerboard on tabletop, creating 64 equal-size squares. Mask off outer edge of checkerboard; paint the outer area blue. Paint tabletop edges white. Paint checkerboard red and white.

Measure and cut strips of thin yellow rickrack to frame and divide the checkerboard and to frame drawer fronts. Adhere rickrack with tacky glue; let dry. Screw small hooks into the underside of tabletop to hold small items.

Industrial Chic

Paint the table and drawers midnight blue. Let dry. Drill hole in the center of each drawer front to accept carriage bolt pulls. Wear gloves and use wire cutters to cut aluminum screen to fit the tabletop and the drawer fronts; allow extra to wrap screen around the edges of the tabletop and the drawer fronts. Staple the screen edges to the underside of the tabletop and the back side of the drawers. Fold screen corners like gift wrap.

Using wire cutters, snip an X in the screen covering each hole in the drawer fronts. Slip in bolt. Use a nut inside the drawer and one outside to tighten bolt in place. Repeat for other drawer.

Cut square wood dowel to fit tabletop along back edge and side edges. Paint dowel black; let dry. Secure with finishing nails. Hot-glue acorn nuts to dowels as shown.

Screw angle brackets to legs, positioning the pairs as shown. Paint the space between pairs black.

131

Finessed from Fabric

STYLE LESSON: Fabric inspires color and style.
BACKGROUND: In this fashionable family room, floral fabric serves as Laurie's muse for a contemporary makeover that includes a handsome storage and display wall.

From the Floral ◄

Focused on the goal of making the family room both beautiful and functional for multiple activities, Laurie pulls her palette from a stylized floral-pattern fabric, which she uses for pillows and for the top of an ottoman slipcover. Colors from the fabric climb the walls: Buttery yellow brings in sunshine, and horizontal orange stripes top off the space with contemporary appeal. Creamy white paint refreshes the fireplace. Laurie clears clutter from the setting by adding a wall of storage. A single row of open shelving continues the line of the orange stripes; enclosed cabinets below keep the television and other items out of sight. Laurie even makes room at the bottom of the cabinets for dog beds. "That's their Hide-A-Bed," Laurie says, smiling.

Have a Seat ▲

An off-white slipcover for the sofa is a subtle background that allows an assortment of orange, green, and floral pillows to pop. Artwork above the sofa emphasizes the color palette. A pair of chrome-arm chairs, reupholstered in touchable green fabric, introduces a fun, retro element to the room. To accommodate a radiator, the built-in below the open shelf on this side of the doorway doesn't open, but offers symmetry to the space.

Before You Go... ▼

Because this family room is open to a kitchen, Laurie also renewed a section of damaged countertop between the spaces. For a temporary but functional cover-up, she wrapped the countertop with this heavy-duty vinyl in mustard yellow to complement the walls. Decorative nailhead trim keeps the vinyl in place and adds an attractive detail. *For more information on nailhead trim, turn to page 115.*

133

Measuring Accurately

Quality results depend on quality measuring tools and sound techniques.

An old woodworker's maxim—measure twice; cut once—couldn't be truer. Use these super-simple tips for measuring and cutting more accurately.

A **V marks the spot.** A single, wobbly mark where you want to cut could cause problems. You may forget which end of the line marks the cut. A thick line from a blunt pencil could cause a misfit too. Instead, mark where you want to cut with a V, placing the point precisely on the spot.

B **Remember blade thickness.** When you cut a board, the blade cuts away about ⅛ inch of the lumber. To account for the thickness, mark the waste side of the cutoff line with an X; position your saw on the waste side of the mark.

C **When cutting more than one length from a single board,** make double marks to compensate for the saw kerf. Otherwise, each subsequent piece will be too short.

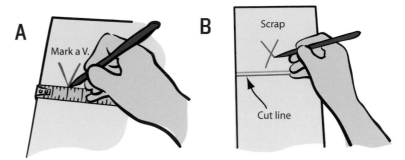

A — Mark a V.

B — Scrap / Cut line

C — Mark a double line to allow for saw kerf.

In some instances, such as when finding the inside dimensions of a cabinet, a folding ruler with a slide-out metal piece will provide the most accurate and accessible means for obtaining the measurements.

Measuring Tape

Inch by inch, foot by foot, good measuring tools make the difference.

No toolbox is complete without a steel tape measure. Tapes are available in two types of cases: plastic, which is lightweight, and metal, which is sturdy. For best accuracy, purchase a tape with a hook on the end that slides forward or backward (see illustration, *right*). When measuring a board for an outside dimension, slide the hook forward to compensate for the thickness of the hook itself. When taking an inside measurement—such as a cabinet interior—slide the hook back to begin measuring at true zero. Two handy features are a lock mechanism, to hold the tape in place while you take a measurement, and a spring return, which automatically winds the tape back into the case. Choose a tape that's long enough for typical measuring jobs around your house. Also, consider selecting a model with both metric and imperial scales so the tape can allow you to easily convert measurements when needed. For precision, look for a tape with ¹⁄₃₂ grads over the first 12 inches of the tape.

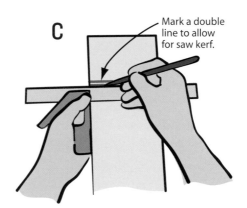

A Favorite for Feet

Comfortable, stylish, and colorful, ottomans are gaining in popularity, turning up in living rooms, family rooms, bedrooms, and baths.

Go basic. To build an ottoman, cut wood and foam to size. Set the foam on top of the wood and wrap the two pieces in fabric, stapling the fabric to the wood. Attach legs to wood base. In an Orlando living room, Laurie covered a square ottoman in harvest-tinted fabric and rested the piece on button legs.

Embellish for added style. Ottomans can be as elegant as any other piece of furniture. Sew on buttons or tassels for a personalized look. Or add beaded, fabric, or nailhead trim to the seams or skirting for a finished touch. In Colorado: Berry Avenue, Hildi tufted an ottoman by adding fabric-covered buttons pulled tightly through the foam and wood bottom of the piece.

Choose funky shapes. Furniture stores sell round, oval, and asymmetrical ottomans. For a custom look, cut wood and foam to any shape and then cover with fabric. Add legs as needed. In a fraternity house, Doug built two circular ottomans covered in quadrants with orange and green fabric.

Boost the functionality. Ottomans often get used as coffee tables, so consider combining two purposes in one piece. Build, purchase, or customize combination seating/table furniture that offers casual flexibility. In Austin, Hildi built a combination coffee table/ottoman. One half featured slate tile; the other side was covered with a green chenille cushion.

Slipcover for new life. If you love the size and shape of an ottoman but hate the style of the fabric, reupholster or slipcover the piece. Online and print catalog resources offer a variety of slipcover options, including covers for ottomans. In an Indianapolis living room, Gen re-covered a large existing ottoman with repurposed fabric from an old sofa slipcover.

SO SMILE ALREADY

136

Chapter 8: So Smile Already The world would be a sorry place without laughter. That's why you'll often see *Trading Spaces* designers including fun and humorous touches in many of their rooms. So go ahead, look around, laugh a little... and feel free to take some happiness home.

DICKERSON

A Night Under the Stars

STYLE LESSON: Choose kid-friendly themes that have room to grow.
BACKGROUND: Hildi looks to the great outdoors for inspiration for an adventurous boy's bedroom. The night sky, a golden moon, and glowing stars overlook a tented sleeping area and a rock-climbing wall.

A Theme to Dream Under ◀

Let yourself go when decorating a child's room: Go bold; go distinctive—go thematic. The great outdoors is Hildi's theme in this boy's room. She uses a blue and gray tent as an oversize canopy, marking off a snug sleeping hideaway. The shiny blue comforter is actually a sleeping bag unzipped and opened flat. To stretch your budget, look for a tent and other supplies at an army surplus store or secondhand shop.

Wish Upon a Star ▼

Even if it's raining outdoors, the stars are always out, and the moon is always shining in this bedroom. Blue paint, in a shade reminiscent of a cloudless night sky, offers the perfect foil for constellations of stick-on glow-in-the-dark stars and a golden moon light fixture near the ceiling peak.

To learn how to replace a ceiling light fixture, turn to page 142.

Other Worlds ▼

A trip to a specialty store yielded a solar system of cool colored orbs. Most museum gift shops carry models of the planets. Or check local hobby shops or online stores to nab out-of-this-world accessories. If you're feeling creative, make your own solar system: Use foam spheres from a crafts store and decorate them with crafts paint and glitter.

Style Cues Make a kid's passion your decorating inspiration.

Not all children love camping, of course. Fashion your child's theme room to reflect his or her favorite activities, movies, or books. A young girl who loves princesses and knights might enjoy a bed constructed atop high posts and sheathed in plywood cut and painted to resemble a castle. The space below the bed can be a playhouse. For a kid who loves basketball, peel up the carpet, paint the floor as a minicourt, and hang a hoop. Create a plywood "press box" that's big enough to hold the bed and bring in painted lockers for storage. Make a scoreboard and use mailbox numbers for keeping score.

139

Stud Finder

Choose this handy tool to help hang heavy objects safely.

Weighty artwork can hang practically anywhere on a wall with the aid of special anchors, but sometimes you absolutely need to drive a nail or screw into a wall stud, such as when you're hanging a large mirror, wood planking, or bench seating. Use these tips to locate wall studs:

1. Most wall studs occur every 16 or 24 inches along a wall; the distance is measured from the center of one stud to the next. Older homes can be more irregular.

2. Drywall and baseboard moldings are secured to studs, so look for signs of seams, nails, or screws that can indicate the location of a stud.

3. Rap lightly on the wall with your knuckles. The wall sounds more solid over a stud and hollow over the space between studs.

4. Hardware stores sell electronic and magnetic devices that locate the studs for you. Buy one for the toolbox.

Rather than giving every surface in the room a theme treatment, add thematic accessories to a basic, neutral backdrop of wall and accent colors. To switch to a new theme, swap out a few furnishings and add some new accents.

● ●

Because It's There ◀

Most kids love to climb, and the 13-foot-tall peak in this room provides the perfect vertical surface for a rock-climbing wall. Plastic rocks offer handholds to finish the wall. Look for screw-on handholds that resemble real rocks at specialty stores for rock-climbing enthusiasts or check out online resources. A knotted rope, bolted to a beam at the ceiling peak, offers yet another way to reach the top.

Collapsible Design ▲

Inside the tent, two inflatable mattresses team up with the regular bed to handle extra campers for sleepovers. Drag the inflatables out of the tent when climbers need a safe landing spot. A folding camp stool doubles as a

bedside table, and a portable fluorescent lantern sheds light for reading and late nights of telling spooky tales.

A Way with Wood ▲

Sheets of birch plywood secured to framing studs and painted with a stylized rock motif give the room a warm yet graphic look. The free-form, hand-painted rocks feature several shades of gray for a convincing three-dimensional look. Applying a clear coating to the painted paneling allows the wood grain to show through in the spaces between the rocks. Rock formations could also be stenciled on. *For information on buying plywood and MDF, see page 14. For tips on cutting plywood, see page 16.*

141

Replace a Ceiling Fixture

Lighten and brighten any space with a new overhead fixture.

For a finished effect, select ceiling fixtures that complement the new look of the room you've remodeled. (P.S.: The following directions also apply to new ceiling fans.)

To do this job, you'll need a voltage tester (available at hardware and home improvement stores for a few dollars), screwdriver, wire stripper, needlenose pliers, wire nuts, and a ladder.

1 Turn off the power at the main control box. Most control boxes feature labels indicating which switch or fuse operates a particular part of the house, specific outlets, and specific light switches and appliances. (If your control box isn't labeled, you may want to turn off all power to the house using the main switch.) Also turn off the wall switch controlling the light fixture you're working on. Unscrew the wire nuts on the fixture and touch the two leads on the voltage tester to either the exposed red and white wires or the black and white wires. If current is running through wires, the tester will glow. Make sure power is off before proceeding.

2 Disconnect the old fixture. Examine how it attaches to the ceiling. Lightweight fixtures typically secure with bolts to a metal strap (A); heavier fixtures usually have a stud-and-hickey mount (C). If the new and old fixtures require different types of mountings, purchase or gather all the needed parts before proceeding.

3 For strap-mount fixtures, reuse the existing strap if possible. Use a wire stripper (B) to remove 1 inch of insulation from the wire leads on the new fixture. Twist any bare strands of wire together. Proceed to Step 5.

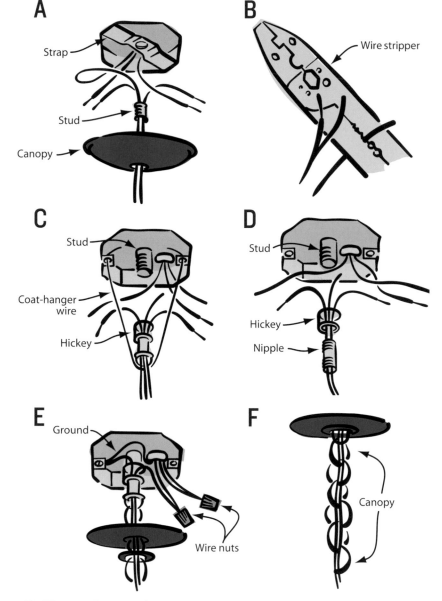

4 For stud-and-hickey mounts, temporarily support the new fixture by hanging it with a coat-hanger wire from the ceiling mount (C). Screw a nipple into the hickey; wires exit through the side of the hickey (D).

5 Thread the hickey onto the stud, or screw the bolt into the strap to mechanically secure the new fixture.

6 Connect matching wires by twisting plastic-coated wire nuts around the wire ends until tight (E). Gently push the wires up and inside the box in the ceiling. Turn on the power at the main control box and light switch. If the fixture works, the connection is good. Turn off the power again at the main control box and secure the canopy to the ceiling (F).

The Light Stuff

Custom ceiling fixtures have what it takes to be winners.

Creative overhead light fixtures are a *Trading Spaces* specialty. Here are some bright overhead ideas that you can adapt for your own spaces.

Drill it. The perfect light shade lives inside your kitchen cabinets. Look for beautiful containers that you can easily drill a hole through and then feed a lamp kit through the hole. In Cincinnati: Sturbridge Road, Doug used two silver-color bowls as shades in an Asian-inspired dining room.

Cover it. Use unconventional materials to re-cover conventional shade frames. Wire on trinkets, beads, and other baubles for a custom look. In an elegant living room in Springfield: Sunset Terrace, Vern shaped silver mesh into a basic drum shade and embellished it with beads.

Disguise it. Spray paint and specialty bulbs can update an attractive but dated fixture. Gen revived a thrift store chandelier in New Jersey: Catania Court by spray-painting it silver-white, adding candle-flame bulbs, and attaching several branches on each arm with silver crafts wire.

Surround it. The glow from a regular lightbulb sparkles when it's forced to shine through any other glass or reflective item. For a wine importer's kitchen in Orlando: Lake Katherine, Vern suspended bargain-bin wineglasses in an aluminum frame around a single lightbulb, to scintillating effect.

Repurpose it. Attaching pieces of tinted vellum (semitransparent drafting paper, available in a variety of colors at most art supply stores) to a fixture diffuses and modifies the light. In Los Angeles: Springdale Drive, Vern supplemented a blah halogen chandelier with framed pictures of fish printed on yellow vellum.

143

The homeowners admit their wish list is huge: They want this loft to accommodate homework and hobbies as well as games, a home office, and two computers. Oh, and the beige has got to go.

Before

Fun 'n' Games

Kia unites a multipurpose room with a playful, flexible theme.

STYLE LESSON: Combine form and function for great style.
BACKGROUND: Using a multifunctional design approach, Kia transforms an overworked and underperforming loft space to help it serve the diverse needs of an entire family.

● ●

Multiple Functions, Fashionably ◀

Get the most out of a space by making every furnishing perform double duty. By adding multipurpose furniture and accessories, Kia makes a "junk room" into a functional, fun place to work or

hang out. The challenge was to accommodate games, hobbies, and work in one loft space; super-versatile furniture was the first order of business. Kia and Ty fashioned a tabletop (think of it as a wood slipcover) for an existing foosball table. The new tabletop provides a spot for one homeowner's scrapbooking hobby and also serves as a surface for game-playing or spreading out a work project.

On the floor, wood cubes, topped with upholstered cushions, serve as seating. The cube interiors offer storage for crafts supplies. When not in use, the cubes tuck out of the way beneath the table.

Kia separated the existing L-shape office desk into two work surfaces and positioned the pair side by side, making the loft seem more spacious.

Recycled Style ◀

Kia hot-glued shimmering CDs in rows above the snack bar for a little game-room glamour. Gather up old CDs or computer discs—or purchase a box of blanks—and apply them as futuristic tile on walls, tabletops, and door and drawer fronts.

● ●

When square footage is at a premium, every piece of furniture in a space needs to perform double or triple duty. Choose convertible pieces, such as sleeper sofas and futons, and collapsible tables and chairs.

Pipe Dreams ▲

Kia selected copper tubing parts directly from the plumbing aisle to set up this custom-designed chess game. Male and female connectors, reducers, angled pieces, and stubs play the various roles. Coat one set of copper pieces with clear sealer so they don't tarnish. Spray-paint the opposing set metallic silver or some other finish.

Burning Issues ▲

The new tabletop slipcover is made from birch plywood and can be lifted off the table base—a foosball table—whenever necessary. After drawing 64 same-size squares to form the chessboard grid, Ty and the homeowners used a woodburning tool to highlight the outline of the game board and a blowtorch to darken alternating squares. Create your own custom game-playing surface (for Chinese checkers, backgammon, solitaire, and other games) or enhance the table with helpful measurement guides (for quilting, sewing, and designing stained-glass projects).

A wood slipcover for a tabletop is simply elongated cube construction (see page 148). Use a wood slipcover to conceal an unattractive or worn tabletop—or to make a small table larger or a different shape.

TOOLBOX

Electric Sanders

Make quick work of small- to medium-size sanding jobs with a pistol-grip random-orbit sander, which smoothes rough surfaces without leaving behind swirl marks. Choose a sander that fits comfortably in your hand and is light enough that you can hold it for a few minutes at a time without tiring. Use sandpaper made specifically for your sander and choose the appropriate grit for your project. Sand with the grain of the wood and keep the sander constantly moving in order to avoid an uneven finish.

Get great ideas from games and game boards: The fresh colors, funky graphics, and distinctive playing pieces are sure to inspire a few decorating projects.

REC   PAIGE CAM

Build a Basic Cube

For display, storage, or perhaps something bigger, basic cube construction is a starting point for creating custom furniture that perfectly matches your needs.

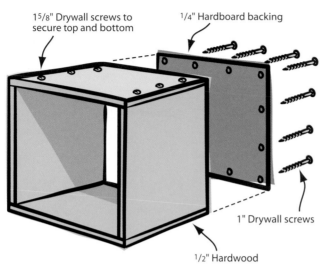

1⁵/₈" Drywall screws to secure top and bottom

1/4" Hardboard backing

1" Drywall screws

1/2" Hardwood

Size the cube according to your needs. For example, a wood tabletop cover is merely a basic cube, sized to the specific dimensions of the table. Cubes of different sizes can be stacked or placed side-by-side to house a stereo, television, and other electronic equipment. For stability, secure cubes to one another as well as to wall studs. To make a cube, cut four pieces of hardwood, plywood, or MDF to the desired lengths and widths for the cube sides. Cut the width of two sides shorter by the thickness of the wood times two. Cut backing from hardboard or use plywood for larger projects that require stronger construction (such as a bed).

Join the side pieces with glue and screws, using simple butt joints. Add backing with glue and screws.

Touch up screw holes with wood filler. Sand the box; then stain it or prime and paint it.

A cube in disguise: The hanging bed frame in Kia's India-inspired bedroom is a custom version of the classic cube. The dimensions accommodate a full-size mattress.

Find the Cube

Glance through the following sampler, and you'll discover that basic cube construction is the foundation for many groovin' designs for custom furniture.

Cubes as end tables. Position a cluster of cubes to allow storage from any angle. Set the cube cluster in the center of a room or on a rotating base for 360 degrees of storage. In a Knoxville living room, Hildi set groupings of four-in-one cubes on lazy Susans to serve as end tables.

Cubes as changeable seating. By adding an upholstered cushion or piece of wood or stone to the top of a cube, you'll create seating that's easy to move and easy to redecorate. In a child's room, Gen added hinged, upholstered tops to four storage cubes and added casters to the underside for mobility.

Cubes as shadow boxes. Think of a cube as a deep picture frame waiting to be filled. Hang a cube on the wall and display books, artwork, toys, or knickknacks on the horizontal ledges created by the cube. In Texas: Sutton Court, Laurie built cubical display cases for the homeowners' dishes.

Cubes as support. Stack an elongated cube on a cube and you have the beginnings of a stable and strong table. To support a heavy tabletop surface, such as a marble slab, or to provide an extra-stable base, build two or more cubes side by side to serve as a base; then add the top. In Nazareth: First Street, Vern built a coffee table by placing a custom surface on a cube.

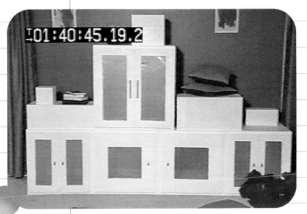

Cubes as an entertainment center. Build a cube or series of cubes to match the dimensions of your home electronics components. Fabricate a few additional cubes to store CDs, DVDs, and other media. Attach all the cubes together for a custom storage unit. Gen configured white cubes (several featuring silver mesh doors) to make a sprawling entertainment unit.

Flower Power

STYLE LESSON: Take a theme to the extreme.
BACKGROUND: Seeking a showstopping wall treatment, Hildi brings in armloads of fabulous fake flowers in all the colors of the rainbow. A new look for the vanity and some creative curtains help transport the homeowners to a floral fantasyland.

Fields of Flowers ◀

When you extend a theme to the extreme, be prepared for dramatic results. Concerned that the existing bathroom wallpaper would be difficult to take down, Hildi dreams up a doable, daring wall cover-up. Armed with nearly 6,000 silk and plastic flowers, Hildi and her homeowners snapped off the blossoms and stapled the flowers—two staples to each one—onto the walls to completely cover the room with colorful, richly textured petals.

"I found flowered fabric in Paris, and it inspired this idea," Hildi explains. "What I always say is focus on one thing, and here my focus was the walls." To bring her flowery vision to fruition, Hildi invested most of her budget on the blossoms—about $600. *To learn more about staple guns—definitely a timesaving tool for this kind of task and many others—* *turn to page 116.*

Gilded and Aglow ▶

To make plain-white cabinetry more elegant, Hildi chose a metallic gold-painted finish and sparkling crystal knobs. Red acrylic panels replace solid-wood centers on each door. A tap light behind each translucent panel adds a pleasing glow that serves as romantic mood lighting or a night-light. *To learn how to remove the center panels from wood cabinet doors and how to cut acrylic* *panels, turn to page 156.*

Before 24

Speaking from a bubble-filled bathtub, the homeowners say their bathroom is too big. Never fear—Hildi is here with armloads of intimacy.

Dress up the most humble of cabinetry with coordinated custom details: Mix and match finishes, inset panel designs, and knob or pull choices to achieve the look you desire.

Take texture one step further for heightened style. For example, forgo linen fabric for burlap or ditch merely shiny surfaces for mirrored ones.

Style, Uninterrupted ▲

The flower theme flows into the tub alcove, and Hildi takes care to keep the rest of the design flowing too. Molding at the ceiling and trim around the window, for example, feature the same gold paint as the cabinetry. Plastic flowers hot-glued to the cafe curtains blend window and wall boundaries.

For information on glue guns, turn to page 28.

Router
Use this versatile tool to create custom finishing touches.

A router is a great tool for giving distinctive, finished looks to wood edges. It's also handy for cutting center panels out of cabinet doors (see page 156 for more information). It can help you round off the edges of a wood or MDF tabletop, make custom moldings and picture frames, or cut grooves and designs into flat surfaces.

For your first handheld router, look for a model with a 1½-hp motor, variable speeds, and a fixed-base bit (a bit that remains stationary; on a plunge router, the bit can be pushed down past the base plate—a feature better suited to more advanced woodworking). As you shop, hold various router styles and brands in your hands and notice which weight and handle grip feels best. Note whether the power trigger or switch is conveniently located. Check out the options for temporarily attaching the router to a stationary surface.

For continuity, Hildi painted the crown molding and door and window casings gold to match the cabinetry. Previously painted moldings and casings should be sanded to rough up any glossy finish. Wipe away the sanding residue with a tack cloth; then apply a coat of primer. Once dry, paint the moldings as desired. Semigloss or gloss finishes hold up best in high-use areas.

REC

Modesty Makeover ▲

To give the glass shower more privacy in this mirror-wrapped room, Hildi extends beautiful
floral fabric from the floor to the 10-foot-high ceiling around one end of the stall, integrating
the relatively short shower stall (only 6 feet tall) with the spaciousness of the room.
   Lavender paint on the ceiling serves, Hildi says, as an "interpretation of the sky."

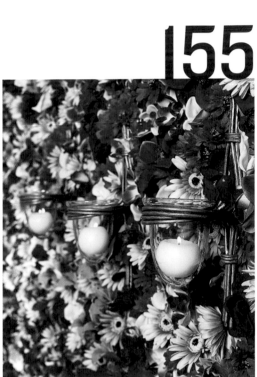

Bench Beautiful ▲

Extra-thick legs give this custom-made oval bench a substantial feel; the curved feet add a feminine touch. Serving as a cushion cover, a white terry cloth towel is wrapped around the foam-and-batting-covered plywood oval and stapled to the back of the wood. "Staple the ends, then the sides," Hildi says. "If you work around the perimeter, you end up with the fabric bunched up."

Mood Lighting ▲

No luxury bathroom is complete without the soft glow of candles. This trio of gold wire and glass wall sconces keeps the flickering flames away from the flower-covered walls.

The process of upholstering a bench seat is similar to upholstering a headboard. Find out more about basic upholstery techniques by turning to page 116.

Cabinet-Painting Tips
For beautiful results, take a peek at these tips.

To ensure that your cabinet-painting projects come out as wonderful as you hope, wear rubber gloves and goggles and clean the cabinet surfaces with TSP (trisodium phosphate), a cleaning agent available at home and hardware stores. Rinse well and let dry.

Lightly sand the surfaces. (Hildi's homeowners initially skipped this step, and the paint didn't stick to the glossy surface.) Wipe clean with a tack cloth. Brush or spray on quality primer. Let dry.

Lightly sand the primed surface if the grain is raised. Wipe clean with a tack cloth. Brush, roll, or spray on the finish color. Apply as many coats as needed to achieve rich, uninterrupted color, allowing each coat to dry according to manufacturer's directions before applying the next coat.

Solid-Panel Substitutes

To give cabinets a whole new look, remove the solid-wood center panel and trade it for other materials, such as decorative metal or glass. Put on safety goggles and follow these tips:

1
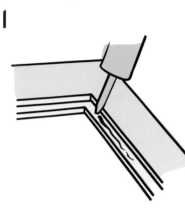

2

3
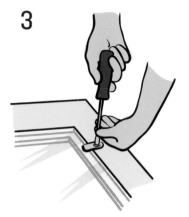

After taking the cabinet door off the hinges, use a handheld router equipped with a plunge-cut bit and cut out the center wood panel. Be careful not to cut through the rabbet, or lip, if the panel rests on one. Remove the panel. If the door frame lacks a rabbet for the new insert to rest on, equip the router with a rabbet bit. Cut a lip all the way around the inside perimeter of the door frame. Cut glass, metal, acrylic sheeting, mesh, fabric or other insert material so that it will fit within the frame and rest on the rabbet.

BApply a bead of clear silicone caulk on the rabbet, all the way around the frame. Press glass, metal, or other material in place.

CSecure glass inserts with mirror clips around the inside perimeter. To secure other materials, use a stapler or small brads. Or, in lieu of cutting a rabbet around the back of the door frame, simply secure the glass panel directly to the back of the door frame using clear silicone caulk and mirror clips. When applying other materials, such as a woven mat, wire grid, or decorative metal, use staples and a staple gun, U-nails, or small brads to secure the material to the back of the door frame.

Never clean acrylic with sprays formulated for glass. Also avoid scouring compounds. Instead, clean with a soft cloth, water, and a mild detergent or soap. Thoroughly rinse the surface and dry with a soft, dry cloth.

Cutting Acrylic

Always leave the plastic film on the acrylic sheet while you make cuts. For straight cuts, use a handheld tool designed for cutting plastic. Position a straightedge where you want to cut, and score the plastic with the cutting tool. Make several passes with the cutting tool to deepen the score line.

Align the score line along a table edge; then position the straightedge on top of the sheet and align with the score line. While pressing down on the straightedge, press downward on the overhanging portion of the sheet. The acrylic will snap along the score line.

You can also make straight cuts using a table saw equipped with a blade designed for cutting acrylic.

After making cuts, lightly sand the cut edge smooth.

Cabinet Charisma

There's more than one way to dress up ordinary wood storage.

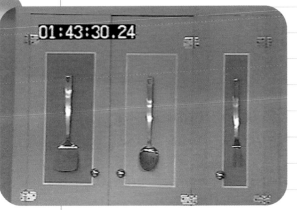

Add metallic luster. Sure, new knobs or handles can refresh a bank of cabinets, but so can new metallic accents applied to door insets, trim moldings, or hinges. In Knoxville: Stubbs Bluff, Doug painted kitchen cabinet fronts sage green and lavender and then hung various silver kitchen utensils in the center of each panel.

Insert some texture. For a dramatic dash of visual interest, replace stained or painted insets with pieces of metal screen, radiator covers, chicken wire, shirred-on fabric panels, or other materials. In Austin: Wing Road, Gen removed cabinet centers and replaced them with sheets of patterned tin.

Put your stuff on display. Artfully arrange everyday kitchen supplies. Open shelving or glass doors let you showcase dishware, glassware, colorful baking supplies, or gleaming appliances. In her artichoke-themed kitchen, Gen cut out wood door insets and replaced them with clear acrylic.

Paint on some accents. Apply touches of contrasting color to cabinetry. Paint wiggly lines, vines, flowers, or polka dots for the best effect. If freehand painting isn't your strength, consider using a stencil to guide your embellishing. In an Austin kitchen, Doug painted purple swirls on cream-color cabinets.

Start with doors in mind. Purchase doors or frames from antiques shops, home centers, or crafts stores and build a cabinet to fit the doors. In a New York bedroom, Vern built a cube shelving unit, using the dimensions of picture frames as a guide. The frames were filled with drawings and photos and attached to the unit with hinges to serve as doors.

episode guide

Think you're the ultimate *Trading Spaces* fan? Prove it by rating the room redos of every episode of the show in this handy-dandy listing guide.

This complete, chronological tour through the years with your favorite decorating show is so chock-full of facts, figures, and funnies that even die-hard fans will learn a thing or two! Check out the Icon Legend below to help locate episodes with High Stress Alerts, Tearjerker Reactions, and more. And don't forget to record your opinion of each and every transformation by using the super-easy ☺ ☺ ☹ Smiley Face scale.

158

💣 = Demolition   ☹ = Tearjerker   ✹ = Ceiling Fan   😲 = Stress Alert   🖌 = Homeowners with Power Tools

⊣▥ = Paint Explosion   ⑦ = What Were They Thinking?   ⟶◀ = Carpenter to the Rescue   Ⓢ = Budget Crisis   ♥ = Fan Favorite

Season 1

Knoxville: Fourth & Gill

Cast: Alex, Frank, Laurie, Amy Wynn

The Rooms: In the premiere episode, Frank brightens a den by using a faux-suede finish in shades of gold on the walls, reupholstering the homeowners' Arts and Crafts furniture, and painting two armoires in shades of red, gold, and black. Laurie punches up a bland kitchen by painting the walls electric pear, retiling the floor in large black and white checks, and using chrome accents. She also creates an organized family message and filing center.

Watch For: Frank demonstrates the "Frank Droop," meant to keep your arm from getting tired while painting. (It's a shoulder shimmy crossed with a slight back bend.)

Budget Note: Both Frank and Laurie are under budget, but host Alex never even mentions the fact during the end Designer Chat segment.

Frank's Room: ☺ ☺ ☹
Laurie's Room: ☺ ☺ ☹

Knoxville: Forest Glen ☹ 😲

Cast: Alex, Doug, Hildi, Amy Wynn

The Rooms: Doug creates a romantic bedroom, which he titles "Country Urbane," by painting the walls sage green, building an upholstered bed, pickling an existing vanity, and making a privacy screen. Hildi designs a sleek living room, painting the walls a dark putty, sewing white slipcovers and curtains, hanging spotlights on the walls to showcase the homeowners' art, and building end tables that spin on lazy Susans.

Fashion Report: Doug wears dark, angular glasses and has curly hair.

Notable: On his first episode, Doug throws a couple of low-voltage diva fits: one in which he paces and repeatedly mumbles "Why stress tomorrow when you can stress today?" and another in which he walks off-camera and screams.

Crisis: Hildi creates controversy by wanting to paint a thin black stripe around the edge of the wood floor. Her homeowners hate the idea and refuse to take any part in it. She and Alex eventually do it.

Reveal-ing Moment: One of the living room homeowners starts to cry unhappy tears and exclaims, "Oh my God! They painted my floor!"

Doug's Room: ☺ ☺ ☹
Hildi's Room: ☺ ☺ ☹

Athens: County Road ☹ ✹

Cast: Alex, Frank, Hildi, Amy Wynn

The Rooms: Frank brightens a child's room by painting the walls lavender, hanging a swing from the ceiling, making a wall-size art area with chalkboard spray paint, and spray-painting a mural of white trees. Hildi updates a kitchen/living room area by painting the dark wood paneling and ceiling ecru, hanging cream draperies, slipcovering chairs with monkey-print fabric, building shelves to showcase the homeowners' pewter collection, and painting several pieces of furniture black.

Safety First: When Frank's female homeowner won't tie her hair back while spackling, he tells her that his hair is gone because of a bad spackling incident.

Hurry Up!: Frank falls way behind on Day 2, so Alex takes the AlexCam to a retirement community and gets shots of seniors saying that they've heard Frank might not finish on time.

Quotable Quote: One of Hildi's homeowners must not know her very well; she tells Hildi, "You could've lived in pioneer times."

Frank's Room: ☺ ☺ ☹
Hildi's Room: ☺ ☺ ☹

Alpharetta: Providence Oaks

Cast: Alex, Hildi, Roderick, Amy Wynn

The Rooms: Hildi re-creates a dining room using the existing dining table, aubergine paint, pistachio curtains, two-tone slipcovers, a striking star-shape light fixture, and a privacy screen. Roderick brightens a den/guest room by painting off-white stripes on the existing khaki walls, stenciling a sun motif in a deep rust-red, slipcovering the furniture with an off-white fabric, and installing a wall-length desk that can be hidden with curtains.

Yucky Moment: Amy Wynn holds a pencil between her toes while measuring out the desk unit with Roderick.

Time Waster: Hildi, Alex, and Hildi's homeowners search for two days to find china—digging in the attic and asking the other homeowners where they store it—so they can set the table for the end shot. They never find it.

Notable: Although he's never seen again on the show, Roderick is the first designer to use the term "homework" while talking to the homeowners about what needs to be done before the next morning. However, this is not the standard "homework assignment" scene that appears in later episodes.

Hildi's Room: ☺ ☺ ☹
Roderick's Room: ☺ ☺ ☹

Lawrenceville: Pine Lane 💣 🖌 ☹

Cast: Alex, Dez, Hildi, Amy Wynn

The Rooms: Dez adds a feminine touch to a dark wood-paneled living room by whitewashing the walls, painting the fireplace, and dismantling a banister. She finds new ways to display the husband's taxidermy and decoy duck collection, including creating a custom duck lamp. Hildi brings the outdoors in, creating an organically hip living room with a tree limb valance, wicker furniture, minty-white walls, and an armoire covered with dried leaves.

Paint Problems: One of Dez's homeowners apparently spends both days priming and painting one built-in bookcase. His excuse: "Paint dries on its own time."

Wonder Woman: Amy Wynn demolishes Dez's banister seemingly with her bare hands.

Notable: Hildi offers a tired Dez some advice at the end of Day I: "Delegate, delegate, delegate."

Dez's Room: ☺ ☺ ☹
Hildi's Room: ☺ ☺ ☹

Buckhead: Canter Road 💣

Cast: Alex, Genevieve, Laurie, Amy Wynn

The Rooms: Gen gets wild in a kitchen by painting the walls electric pear, adding silver accents, using colanders as light covers, and removing cabinet doors. Laurie creates a crisp living room by painting the walls chocolate brown, laying a sea-grass rug, and adding cream and white slipcovers and curtains.

Fashion Report: Gen is barefoot the entire episode.

Quotable Quote: Gen wants to change the flooring but doesn't have time. She expresses her disappointment by saying, "Linoleum bites."

Notable: The now famous "Carpenter Consult" scene debuts, with Laurie consulting Amy Wynn.

Gen's Room: ☺ 😐 ☹
Laurie's Room: ☺ 😐 ☹

Washington, DC: Cleveland Park ⍰ ⊣▮

Cast: Alex, Dez, Doug, Ty

The Rooms: Dez creates a funky-festive living room by combining electric pear, white, gray, black, and red paint in solids, stripes, polka dots, and textured faux finishes. Doug goes retro in a basement by making a beanbag sofa and a kidney-shape coffee table and painting the walls bright orange.

Notable: One of Dez's young female homeowners is smitten with Ty and quickly volunteers to work with him on a project, leaving the remaining partner to say to Dez, "Who does she think she's kidding?"

Quotable Quote: One of Doug's homeowners criticizes Doug's free-form planning by saying, "I wish you spent as much time laying this project out as you did on your hair this morning."

Dez's Room: ☺ 😐 ☹
Doug's Room: ☺ 😐 ☹

Alexandria: Riefton Court

Cast: Alex, Frank, Genevieve, Ty

The Rooms: Frank cozies a country kitchen by creating a picket-fence shelving unit and using seven pastel paint colors to create a hand-painted quilt. Gen goes graphic in a living room, blowing up and recropping family photos, turning an existing entertainment center on its side, and painting the walls bright red.

Quotable Quote: Explaining his design, Frank says, "I thought…country quilt. This looks like a quilt threw up in here, but when you see the result, you're gonna love it."

Conflict: Frank questions why Ty is spending more time on Gen's project and less time on the "quilt": "Could it be because [at] the other house the individual is very tall, very gorgeous, and has enough sex appeal to knock over a troupe?"

Frank's Room: ☺ 😐 ☹
Gen's Room: ☺ 😐 ☹

Annapolis: Fox Hollow

Cast: Alex, Genevieve, Laurie, Ty

The Rooms: Gen warms a living room with butterscotch paint, white curtains, framed family pictures, and a combination wood/carpet floor. Laurie cleans a drab kitchen with muted pumpkin paint, new light fixtures, and a custom pot hanger.

Notable: Gen leads morning stretches with her homeowners before getting to work on Day 2. Laurie removes her first ceiling fan on the show.

Gen's Room: ☺ 😐 ☹
Laurie's Room: ☺ 😐 ☹

Philadelphia: Strathmore Road

Cast: Alex, Frank, Dez, Amy Wynn

The Rooms: Frank goes earthy by painting a living room brown with a sueding technique. He also creates a window seat with storage, handmade accents, and a child-size tepee. Dez tries for "casual elegance" in a living room, using purple paint, a repeated gray harlequin pattern on the walls, and an end table lamp made out of a trash can.

Quotable Quotes: Frank trying to figure out how comfortable a cushion is: "What's the heinie quotient on that?" Frank running out of time on Day 2: "I'm so tense…you could literally use me as a paper press."

Oops!: Frank is 23 cents over budget.

Reveal-ing Moment: The homeowners hate Dez's room with a vengeance, stating "We've got the set of The Dating

Game on our walls" and "Beetlejuice lives here."

Frank's Room: ☺ 😐 ☹
Dez's Room: ☺ 😐 ☹

Philadelphia: Valley Road

Cast: Alex, Doug, Laurie, Amy Wynn

The Rooms: Doug softens a sunroom he names "Blue Lagoon" by painting the walls a deep robin's egg blue, painting blue and white diamonds on the hardwood floor, hanging whitewashed bamboo blinds, and adding pale yellow accents. Laurie goes Greek, painting a living room deep russet with black and white accents, adding white Grecian urns, and creating a white bust using one of her homeowners as a model.

Yucky Moment: Doug uses picture wire as dental floss.

Notable: Laurie thinks she's so ahead of schedule on Day 1 that she leads Doug to believe she's been asked to slow down and relax with the family dog so as not to finish too early. She then falls quite behind on Day 2 and becomes very stressed about finishing.

Doug's Room: ☺ 😐 ☹
Laurie's Room: ☺ 😐 ☹

Philadelphia: Galahad Road

Cast: Alex, Hildi, Genevieve, Amy Wynn

The Rooms: Hildi warms a family-friendly living/dining room by introducing coffee-color walls, a midnight blue fireplace, a custom-built sectional couch, and zebra-stripe dining chair covers. Gen brightens a basement den by painting the walls lily pad green, adding orange accents, installing a white modern couch, and weaving white fabric on the ceiling to cover the drop-ceiling tiles.

Fashion Report: Gen wears a cowboy hat the entire episode.

Wise Wynn: Gen plans to demolish an entire wall, but Amy Wynn talks her out of it due to structural concerns.

Wicked Wynn: Amy Wynn tells Alex that the coffee table she's constructing for Gen is "really, really ugly" and that she'd throw it out if it were in her room.

Hildi's Room: ☺ 😐 ☹
Gen's Room: ☺ 😐 ☹

Knoxville: Courtney Oak ✳

Cast: Alex, Frank, Laurie, Amy Wynn

The Rooms: Frank gets in touch with his "inner child" by painting the walls of a basement light denim blue, free-handing murals of trees and flowers, and spray-painting fluffy white clouds. Laurie goes organic by painting a bedroom a deep pistachio green, adding soft draperies, painting a vine around the vanity mirror, and using a cornice board to drape fabric on either side of the headboard.

Fan Debates: Laurie removes another ceiling fan. Alex argues with Frank about his decision to leave two brown ceiling fans in place. Frank defends his choice: "With people dying everywhere and starving children, really, two ceiling fans of the wrong color are minor trivialities."

Quotable Quotes: Frank to Alex: "I would never beat you. You're a nice person, even though you ask some pointed and completely ugly questions."

Frank's Room: ☺ 😐 ☹
Laurie's Room: ☺ 😐 ☹

Cincinnati: Melrose Avenue

Cast: Alex, Hildi, Frank, Ty

The Rooms: Frank adds soft Victorian touches to a living room by exposing the existing wood floor, creating a faux-tin fireplace surround, painting a navy wall border with a rose motif, creating a fireplace screen that matches the border, and building a bench-style coffee table. Hildi gets crafty in a kitchen, creating her own wallpaper with tissue paper and flower stencils. She installs a dishwasher, extends the countertop, builds an island out of the kitchen

table, paints the ceiling and the furniture yellow, and lays vinyl tile flooring.

Love Connection?: Frank's male and female homeowners admit to crushes on Alex and Ty, respectively.

Notable: Frank admits to country-and-western dancing with his wife.

Hildi's Room: ☺ 😐 ☹
Frank's Room: ☺ 😐 ☹

Cincinnati: Sturbridge Road ☹

Cast: Alex, Genevieve, Doug, Ty

The Rooms: Gen creates an Indian bedroom for a teenage girl by painting the walls with warm golden and red tones, hanging a beaded curtain, and creating a draped canopy. Doug turns a dining room into a "Zen-Buddhist-Asian room" with a chocolate brown ceiling, warm honey-copper walls, randomly placed Venetian plaster squares, and folded-metal-screen window treatments.

Fashion Report: Gen and her homeowners wear Indian forehead markings on both days for inspiration.

Quotable Quote: Gen calls Doug a "weasel" for usurping some of her lumber and states, "I think he's feeling insecure about his room or he's got a little crush on me and he's just really sad about the rejection."

Scary Stuff: Doug raps.

Notable: Doug gives the first official homework assignment on the show.

Gen's Room: ☺ 😐 ☹
Doug's Room: ☺ 😐 ☹

Cincinnati: Madison & Forest ☹ ✳

Cast: Alex, Doug, Laurie, Ty

The Rooms: Doug transforms a Victorian living room into an industrial loft with multiple shades of purple paint, a yellow ceiling, custom art made from coordinating paint chips, wall sconces made of candy dishes, and a chair reupholstered in Holstein fabric. Laurie warms a tiny bedroom with mustard yellow paint, a custom-built entertainment center, and a short suspended bed canopy.

Hurry Up!: Doug has his homeowners create art projects in a 10-minute time frame. Alex walks around with a stopwatch.

Doug's Room: ☺ 😐 ☹
Laurie's Room: ☺ 😐 ☹

San Diego: Elm Ridge $ ⍰ ♥

Cast: Alex, Genevieve, Hildi, Amy Wynn

The Rooms: In this infamous episode, Gen truly brings the outdoors in: She covers a bedroom wall with Oregon moss, lays a natural-tone tile floor, and adds a canopy that is lit from above with twinkling lights. Hildi works to convince her homeowners that they can brighten a bedroom by painting the walls and furniture black, adding zebra-stripe floor cubes, and using exposed subflooring in place of carpet.

Un-bear-able: One of Gen's male homeowners constantly carries around a teddy bear.

Yucky Moment: One of Gen's homeowners complains that the moss wall "smells like somebody's old underwear."

Tile Hell: Due to time constraints, Gen chooses to lay floor tiles with liquid nails instead of adhesive and grout. Her team ends up re-laying many tiles during Day 2 because the adhesive doesn't quite work. Hildi's grout unexpectedly dries white and looks terrible next to dark concrete tiles. Hildi improvises by going over budget and buying rugs.

Busted: Hildi creates a copper mesh bust using herself as a model. The female homeowner isn't thrilled with the idea and says, "You went to design school?"

Gen's Room: ☺ 😐 ☹
Hildi's Room: ☺ 😐 ☹

159

San Diego: Hermes Avenue 💲

Cast: Alex, Laurie, Genevieve, Amy Wynn

The Rooms: Laurie brightens a kitchen by painting the walls Tiffany-box blue, hanging butter yellow draperies, building a banquette seating area, coating the stove in chrome-colored paint, and painting the cabinets butter yellow. Gen uses Georgia O'Keeffe's Southwestern paintings as inspiration for transforming a living room. She paints the walls clay red, hangs a cow skull above the fireplace, adds a woven rug, hangs new light fixtures, frames large black and white cropped photos of the homeowners' children, builds a distressed coffee table with firewood legs, and covers the existing baby bumpers with crafts fur.

Oops!: Gen accidentally steps into a bucket full of spackling compound and must hop around on one foot until one of her homeowners brings her a towel.

Budget Buster: Laurie can't afford to spend money on cabinet hardware, so her homeowners ask for permission to buy it themselves as a gift for their friends. Laurie agrees. During Designer Chat, Alex says that she'll bend the rules once for Laurie, but never again.

Reveal-ing Moment: The female living room homeowner is so excited about her room that she picks up Alex—twice.

Laurie's Room: 😊 😐 ☹️
Gen's Room: 😊 😐 ☹️

San Diego: Wilbur Street

Cast: Alex, Frank, Doug, Amy Wynn

The Rooms: Frank mixes British Colonial and tropical looks in a living room using soft mauve paint, exposed wood flooring, several flowerpots and vases, and a custom architectural piece. Doug updates a dark kitchen with a "Tuscan Today" theme, using Venetian plaster tinted "Tuscan Mango" (OK, it's orange), painting the cabinets white and orange, and installing wood flooring.

Quotable Quotes: Frank-isms abound in this episode. Frank on his wall hanging: "OK, now we're gonna make a metal taco." Frank on how tired he feels: "If someone invited me out to dinner, I'd have to hire someone to chew my food." And Frank on his finished room: "You could get malaria in this room it's so tropical."

Ouch!: Alex helps Frank hot-glue moss to flowerpots and manages to lay her entire palm on a freshly glued spot. She gets hot glue and moss stuck to her hand, and Frank runs off to find first aid.

Frank's Room: 😊 😐 ☹️
Doug's Room: 😊 😐 ☹️

Knoxville: Stubbs Bluff

Cast: Alex, Frank, Doug, Ty

The Rooms: Doug brings a farmhouse kitchen up-to-date by painting the walls a muted coffee color, adding sage and lilac accents, building benches in the dining area, painting the cabinets, and laying vinyl tile. Frank lets the ideas flow while punching up a basement with a karaoke stage, a tiki hut bar, and several other tropical accents—including a canoe for seating.

Oops!: Even though Doug and Alex spend much of the episode mixing plaster to coat a shovel and a pitchfork to hang on the wall, the plaster won't dry fast enough, so Doug ends up spray-painting the tools instead.

Fashion Report: Frank wears a hula outfit—complete with coconut bra—and asks, "Am I showing too much cleavage?"

Quotable Quote: Frank disses Ty's mellow attitude, saying "He goes through like life's little pixie, like a little gnome looking for a mushroom."

Yucky Moment: Frank gnaws off a tree branch with his teeth.

Frank's Room: 😊 😐 ☹️
Doug's Room: 😊 😐 ☹️

Miami: 168th/83rd Streets ❓ ☹️

Cast: Alex, Laurie, Dez, Ty

The Rooms: Laurie warms up a living room by painting the walls brick red with black and cream accents, building two large bookcases, hanging botanical prints, slipcovering the existing furniture, and using a faux-tortoiseshell finish on a coffee table. Dez adds drama to a bedroom by applying a "pan-Asian ethnic theme" featuring upholstered cornice boards, mosquito netting, and stenciled dragon lampshades.

Conflict: Laurie's homeowners want to install a faux fireplace, and she vetoes it. They keep trying to convince Ty to help them build a square frame and paint logs and a fire on it. They keep putting it in the room, and Laurie keeps removing it.

Notable: Dez falls ill with the flu on Day 2 and spends a lot of time sleeping on a couch. As a result, her team falls behind. Ty jumps in to help finish the room on time.

Fashion Report: Dez wears an amazing large-brimmed hat during Designer Chat. It features black and white spots, fuzzy black trim, and a very tall white feather. She's outdone herself.

Laurie's Room: 😊 😐 ☹️
Dez's Room: 😊 😐 ☹️

Fort Lauderdale: 59th Street ✳️ 🔌

Cast: Alex, Frank, Hildi, Ty

The Rooms: Frank adds "comfortable drama" to a living room, with bright orange textured walls, a mosaic-top coffee table, slipcovered furniture, and a large custom art project. Hildi goes retro in a Fiestaware collector's kitchen by building an acrylic table, adding period chairs, and hanging large globe light fixtures. She also installs a shelving unit to display the homeowner's collection.

Quotable Quote: Frank describes his coffee table design to Ty by saying, "If you were in Pompeii just before Vesuvius erupted and you grabbed a piece of furniture, it would be this table."

Notable: Hildi removes her first ceiling fan.

Fashion Report: Hildi wears a bikini top during the opening segment.

Frank's Room: 😊 😐 ☹️
Hildi's Room: 😊 😐 ☹️

Key West: Elizabeth Street 💲

Cast: Alex, Frank, Genevieve, Ty

The Rooms: Frank adds a Caribbean touch to a living room by painting the walls light blue, adding a hand-painted mermaid, building a telephone table, and laying vinyl tiles. Gen makes a tiny living room appear larger with her "Caribbean Chill" design, which includes magenta walls with lime green accents, a large custom-built sectional sofa, and a wall decoupaged with pages torn from a 100-year-old book.

Conflict: Frank's homeowners take the reins and wind up running the show. (They also bring a blender with them, because they never travel without it.) They don't finish their homework, claiming a neighbor came over with champagne.

Quotable Quote: Frank describes the shifting control of the project as "Bad reception—it goes in and out."

Frank's Room: 😊 😐 ☹️
Gen's Room: 😊 😐 ☹️

Austin: Wycliff 💲 🖌️ 😲

Cast: Alex, Doug, Hildi, Amy Wynn

The Rooms: Doug creates a funky kitchen by painting the cabinets with blue and purple swirls, extending the existing countertop, applying blue and purple vinyl squares on the wall, and hanging numerous clocks (he titles the room "Time Flies"). Hildi adds drama to a dining room by covering the walls with brown felt, papering the ceiling with small, individual red and gold squares, covering the back of an armoire with dried bamboo leaves, and making custom light fixtures.

Time Flies: Doug covers a wall with clocks set for different time zones around the world. When the homeowner asks where the clock batteries are, Doug realizes that he forgot to buy them and that he doesn't have money left to get any.

Oops!: In order to paper the ceiling, one of Hildi's homeowners uses a pneumatic glue sprayer and accidentally glues his mask to his beard.

Doug's Room: 😊 😐 ☹️
Hildi's Room: 😊 😐 ☹️

Austin: Wing Road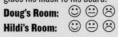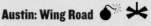

Cast: Alex, Genevieve, Hildi, Amy Wynn

The Rooms: Gen goes south of the border in a kitchen by adding a mosaic tile backsplash, covering the cabinet door insets with textured tin, painting the floors terra-cotta, and painting the walls yellow. Hildi brightens a living room by applying a textured glaze over the existing gold paint, covering a wall in wooden squares, sewing silver slipcovers, and adding a cowhide rug.

Love Notes: Gen's male homeowner has a crush on Amy Wynn.

Fashion Report: Amy Wynn wears two braids à la Laura Ingalls Wilder.

Gen's Room: 😊 😐 ☹️
Hildi's Room: 😊 😐 ☹️

Austin: Birdhouse Drive 🔌

Cast: Alex, Frank, Laurie, Amy Wynn

The Rooms: Frank enlivens a living room by painting three walls sage green, painting the fireplace wall shocking pink, installing floor-to-ceiling shelving on either side of the fireplace, adding a hand-painted checkerboard table, and making unique art pieces. Laurie divides a living/dining room with a suspended piece of fabric, paints the rooms with warm oranges and yellows, adds olive green accents, builds a bench seat, and creates a custom coffee table.

Quotable Quote: Frank describes a wooden rooster he wants to make as "kind of a Frenchy, Mediterranean slash funk Texas rooster."

Time Crunch: During Designer Chat, Laurie confesses that she was running short on time and that the paint on the bench she and Alex are sitting on is still tacky. Laurie freaks a bit because she thinks she's sticking.

Notable: Day 1 is the anniversary of Frank's homeowners. The husband has flowers delivered to his wife, and Frank stays to do their homework that night so the homeowners can go out and celebrate. Oh, and Amy Wynn plays the saw.

Frank's Room: 😊 😐 ☹️
Laurie's Room: 😊 😐 ☹️

Orlando: Lake Catherine

Cast: Alex, Vern, Hildi, Ty

The Rooms: New guy Vern brings warmth and depth into a wine importer's kitchen by painting the walls with two shades of red, installing a custom-built wine rack, building a new chandelier using 36 wineglasses, and creating a new tabletop. Hildi creates a sleek bedroom with gray walls, an aluminum foil ceiling, gray flannel curtains, bamboo curtain rods, and a black armoire covered in bamboo.

Oops!: One of Vern's homeowners juggles lemons and then breaks the vase he's putting them into.

Quotable Quote: When Ty teases Hildi about using too much hair spray, she responds, "Look who's talking, porcupine!"

Tweet Dreams: Hildi includes a live canary in her design and names the bird "Hildi."

Notable: In Vern's premiere episode, viewers are introduced to his perfectionist side: 1) He gives Ty several architectural drawings for what he wants created in the room. 2) After five coats of paint, he and his homeowners are still painting late on Day 2.

Vern's Room: 🙂 😐 🙁
Hildi's Room: 🙂 😐 🙁

Orlando: Gotha Furlong

Cast: Alex, Genevieve, Frank, Ty

The Rooms: Gen creates romance in a bedroom by adding a ceiling-height cedar plank headboard, butter yellow paint, throw pillows made from a 1970s tablecloth, and cedar bookshelves. Frank makes a bedroom feel "earthy, arty, and wonderful" by painting the walls tan, adding gauzy white fabric to the four-poster bed, building a cedar window seat with storage drawers, painting a floorcloth, and hand painting batik-print pillows.

Quotable Quote: Frank says, "You'd better get some popcorn and a good attitude, because this is something you wanna write home to your mother about."

Fashion Report: Ty has an especially bad hair day. Frank paints Alex's nails and says that he does the same for his wife all the time.

Gen's Room: 🙂 😐 🙁
Frank's Room: 🙂 😐 🙁

Orlando: Winterhaven

Cast: Alex, Doug, Laurie, Ty

The Rooms: Laurie perks up a seldom used living room with yellow paint, sheer window treatments, a geometric wall design, and a large ottoman. Doug regresses to his childhood while decorating a boy's bedroom. Doug's design, "Americana Medley," includes red walls, a blue ceiling, stenciled stars and cow prints, a tree limb headboard, and a barn door window treatment.

Mean Streak?: One of Laurie's homeowners is afraid of heights, and Laurie keeps putting him on ladders.

Diva Fit: Doug pouts on the couch because he didn't have his own bedroom growing up.

Quotable Quote: Ty tells Alex that Doug's full name is Douglas "Issues" Wilson.

Doug's Room: 🙂 😐 🙁
Laurie's Room: 🙂 😐 🙁

Albuquerque: Gloria

Cast: Alex, Hildi, Doug, Ty

The Rooms: Hildi warms up a living room by painting the walls brown and copper, applying yellow fabric paint to the existing furniture, making a curtain rod from copper pipe, and installing an entertainment center. Doug sets sail in a living room ("Wind in Our Sails") by painting the walls slate gray, hanging white curtains, installing a banquette, and suspending a large white canvas from the ceiling.

Notable: Alex sings and plays guitar (badly!) for Doug. Doug responds by singing her a song: "Alex is gonna go places we don't want to go. She's gonna be lonely there, singing her sad, sad songs."

Fashion Report: The female homeowners sport blue and green nail polish and nail art that spells out "Trading Spaces."

Hildi's Room: 🙂 😐 🙁
Doug's Room: 🙂 😐 🙁

Santa Fe: Felize

Cast: Alex, Genevieve, Vern, Ty

The Rooms: Gen designs a modern Southwestern living room ("Adobe Mod") by adding white paint, a custom-built sofa, woven-rope end tables, and clay jars. Vern creates a calming oasis in a kitchen by painting the walls pale blue, installing a planter of wheat grass, laying parquet floor, hanging mirrors, and applying a stained-glass look to the cabinet doors.

Notable: Gen's homeowners smudge the room with sage after clearing the furniture from the room.

Yuck!: Vern tastes the wheat grass, hates it, and tries to spit it

out. Alex makes a wheat grass smoothie and hates it too.

Gen's Room: 🙂 😐 🙁
Vern's Room: 🙂 😐 🙁

New Orleans: Jacob Street

Cast: Alex, Laurie, Hildi, Amy Wynn

The Rooms: Laurie connects a kitchen/office/dining/living room, using pale yellow paint on the walls, a 20-foot-long sisal rug, slipcovers, new kitchen storage, and a new furniture arrangement. Hildi modernizes a kitchen by painting the walls pistachio green, laying black vinyl tile, building a new island, and finding new uses for plumbing conduit.

Witchy-Poo: In the spirit of New Orleans, Alex cuts locks of hair from Hildi and Laurie to make voodoo dolls. After making the dolls, Alex sticks each doll in the butt to make the designers hurry up.

Notable: The owners of the multipurpose great-room—both the husband and the wife—cry.

Laurie's Room: 🙂 😐 🙁
Hildi's Room: 🙂 😐 🙁

New Orleans: Walter Road 🔌

Cast: Alex, Genevieve, Frank, Amy Wynn

The Rooms: Gen creates an antique look in a bedroom she titles "Bombay Meets Étouffée." She paints the walls peach and pea green, installs a vintage beaded chandelier, and applies an antique gold finish to cornice boards and bookshelves. Frank updates a kitchen by removing garish wallpaper, coating the walls with textured tan paint, painting cabinet drawers in red and green, coiling copper wire around the existing drawer pulls, and installing a large family bulletin board.

Fashion Report: Gen reveals her numerous fabrics to the homeowners by walking into the room wearing the different cloths around her head, waist, and arms.

Oops!: Frank gets stuck in the pantry while he and his team move the refrigerator; he has to shimmy out a small window.

Huh?: Frank titles his room "Beaver Cleaver Meets George Jetson," but there's no apparent reason why.

Measuring Up: Frank measures a space in a room by lying on the floor and stretching his arms over his head. He tells Amy Wynn the length is "one fat man with arms extended."

Quotable Quote: Frank, on the public's perception of designers: "If somebody tells me that a designer is just this little guy who goes around fluffing flowers, I intend to break every bone in his body and make a lamp out of him."

Gen's Room: 🙂 😐 🙁
Frank's Room: 🙂 😐 🙁

New Orleans: D'evereaux Street 🖌️

Cast: Alex, Vern, Genevieve, Amy Wynn

The Rooms: Vern kicks up the style in a boys' bedroom with a black and white soccer theme. He paints the walls black and white, upholsters the headboards, creates two desk stations, suspends soccer balls from the ceiling, and lays a black and white vinyl floor complete with a custom soccer ball medallion. Gen heads back to the 1960s in her "Retro Fly" den/guest room by painting multicolor stripes on the walls, hanging retro light fixtures, slipcovering an existing futon, and separating the desk area from the seating area with a chain-link screen.

Quotable Quote: Vern consults with the younger boy at the start of the show. Scotty tells Vern he wants to become an architect. Vern gives him a high five and tells him that "Architects get all the women."

Mean Streak?: Alex plays soccer with the two little boys and tells them that the girls at school will love the new "girlie bedroom." The boys knock her to the ground.

Notable: Gen and her homeowners have problems finding wall studs. When their electronic stud finder stops working,

they start drilling random holes to find the studs.

Vern's Room: 🙂 😐 🙁
Gen's Room: 🙂 😐 🙁

New York: Shore Road 🔌 😞 ♥

Cast: Alex, Genevieve, Dez, Amy Wynn

The Rooms: Gen looks to the East for inspiration on a sun porch and creates a tearoom atmosphere with a new sake bar, a seating area, and several organic accents. Dez gives a living room her version of "country with a French twist" by painting the walls yellow, stenciling fern leaves around the room, slipcovering the existing sofa, adding a planter of grass, and hanging geometric window treatments.

Good-Bye: This is Dez's final appearance on *Trading Spaces*.

Oops!: Attempting to shine the sunporch floor, Alex loses control of an electric floor buffer, screams, and eventually falls to the ground.

Oops! Part 2: As Alex huddles near an outdoor fire to get warm, smoke starts to drift toward her, and something gets in her eye. She turns away and complains of being blinded.

Notable: The sunporch homeowners like their room so much, they dance The Monkey.

Gen's Room: 🙂 😐 🙁
Dez's Room: 🙂 😐 🙁

New York: Sherwood Drive

Cast: Alex, Vern, Doug, Amy Wynn

The Rooms: Vern creates a serene bedroom by painting the walls lilac blue, making a television cabinet out of picture frames, hanging yards of indigo velvet, installing sconces containing live Beta fish above the bed, and creating a 4-foot wall clock out of candle sconces and battery-operated clock hands. Doug designs a relaxing "Zen-sational" bedroom by hanging grass cloth on the walls, making light fixtures out of Malaysian baskets, hanging a full-length mirror on an angle, and building a 6-foot fountain.

Conflict: Doug's mother-daughter homeowners tell him that they both have dates and need to stop working at 5 p.m. Doug and Alex explain that the homeowners agreed to complete all the work necessary to redo the room when they signed up for the show. The next morning, the homeowners complain to Doug about the hard work they had to do the night before. However, they don't know that Doug stopped by the previous night and found that they had recruited friends to do their homework for them.

Vern's Room: 🙂 😐 🙁
Doug's Room: 🙂 😐 🙁

New York: Linda Court

Cast: Alex, Doug, Frank, Amy Wynn

The Rooms: Doug creates a Mediterranean-flavored living room by covering the walls in yellow Venetian plaster, making custom lamps, building a large armoire to match an existing one, and weaving strips of wood through metal conduit for a woven-wall effect. Frank also takes the Mediterranean in a living room, applying a faux finish with three shades of yellow paint, then adding stenciled squares on the walls, a faux fresco created from drywall, and gondola-inspired lamps.

Resourceful: Doug's and Frank's designs are so close in concept that Doug sends Alex over to Frank's to borrow some teal and black paint.

Quotable Quote: Alex nags Frank, saying "Time is money!" He responds, "Let me write that down so I can embroider that on a whoopee cushion."

Doug's Room: 🙂 😐 🙁
Frank's Room: 🙂 😐 🙁

161

New Jersey: Sam Street

Cast: Alex, Laurie, Hildi, Ty

The Rooms: Laurie warms up a dining room with yellow paint, shades of berries and pinks as accents, a custom-built cornice board, and cream paint on the existing furniture. Hildi adds drama and romance to a bedroom by painting the walls a yellowed sage green, bringing in several sage silk fabrics, adding a sofa upholstered in burgundy fabric, extending the existing headboard, and building "pillow pod" seating.

Notable: Ty and Alex spend most of the episode running through the woods looking for the legendary Jersey Devil. Laurie does a very bad approximation of a Jersey accent.

Laurie's Room: ☺ ☺ ☹
Hildi's Room: ☺ ☺ ☹

New Jersey: Lincroft 👶 ✻ ☹

Cast: Alex, Laurie, Doug, Ty

The Rooms: Laurie adds style and function to a small kitchen by laying parquet vinyl flooring, painting the walls an ocher yellow, wall-mounting the microwave oven, painting the cabinets white, and creating a home office/family message center. Doug softens a very red living room by painting the walls sandy taupe, adding wooden strips to accentuate the ceiling height, painting colorful checkerboard designs on coffee tables, sewing several brightly colored rag rugs together to create a large carpet, and designing a wooden candleholder using a rope-and-pulley system.

¿Cómo?: Laurie and Ty try to put together a lighting fixture using directions written in Spanish.

Quotable Quote: When Doug's homeowners express concern about the many different accent colors he's using, he responds by saying, "It's not as obnoxious as it could be."

Notable: Alex decides that Doug isn't working fast enough, so she takes over his lamp project. She starts talking to the camera and can't get her pliers open. Doug (in the background) starts doing Alex's job, introducing the episode. He mispronounces things. They decide to keep their regular jobs.

Laurie's Room: ☺ ☺ ☹
Doug's Room: ☺ ☺ ☹

New Jersey: Lafayette Street ✻

Cast: Alex, Frank, Vern, Ty

The Rooms: Frank adds Victorian elements to a dining/living room by painting the walls pink with burgundy accents, showcasing the homeowners' collection of wooden houses, applying decorative molding to the existing entertainment center, and creating original wall art using basic woodcarving skills. Vern softens in a living room, making it baby-friendly. He paints the walls two shades of sage green, builds a large ottoman that doubles as a coffee table, builds a sofa out of a mattress, suspends a mantel for the fireplace, and adds bright blue accents.

Good-Bye: This is Alex's last appearance on *Trading Spaces*.

Swede Thing: Vern attempts to put together an armoire, but the instructions are in Swedish. He convinces Ty to put it together, pointing out that Ty looks more like the man in the illustrations.

Bet Me!: Ty and Alex wager a massage on which designer will finish first. Alex takes Vern, and Ty takes Frank. Both Alex and Ty are underhanded in trying to influence the contest. Ty wins.

Frank's Room: ☺ ☺ ☹
Vern's Room: ☺ ☺ ☹

Season 2

Quakertown: Quaker's Way 👶 ❓ ♥

Cast: Paige, Doug, Hildi, Ty

The Rooms: Doug goes "ball-istic" in a living room, painting the walls lime green, building a custom sofa complete with bowling ball feet, hanging a wall of mirrors, making custom lamps out of gazing balls, and adding brown and blue accents. Hildi introduces viewers to the concept of orthogonal design by painting perpendicular lines on the walls and ceiling of a basement, creating a nine-piece sectional seating area, and screening off a large storage area.

Notable: The Season 2 premiere introduces the graphic opening credits, the outtakes during the end credits, and the *Trading Spaces*/TLC/Banyan Productions trailer outside the carpentry area.

Fashion Report: Ty sports a mustache.

Having a Ball: Doug and Ty steal a gazing ball (for Doug's lamp project) from a neighbor's yard. Ty distracts the neighbor, and Doug runs up and steals the gazing ball. Doug tells Paige during Designer Chat that he returned the stolen ball and purchased similar balls to complete his project.

What Was She Thinking?: Although she knows the homeowners have small children, Hildi makes wall art out of acrylic box frames filled with different types of candy.

Tuneful: Doug plays the sax, Hildi plays the drums, and Ty plays guitar during the opening segment.

Doug's Room: ☺ ☺ ☹
Hildi's Room: ☺ ☺ ☹

New Jersey: Tall Pines Drive 💣💥 ☹ 🖌️

Cast: Paige, Laurie, Vern, Amy Wynn

The Rooms: Laurie experiments with several paint colors in a basement by painting a Matisse-inspired mural. She also makes a chalkboard-top kids' table, installs an art station, creates curtains out of place mats, and hangs louvered panels as a room screen. Vern designs a love nest in a bedroom by hanging brown upholstered wall squares, sewing lush draperies, painting the existing furniture white, installing silver candle chandeliers, and adding new bedside tables.

Yucky Moment: Vern's homeowner loves his design choices so much that she moans as he shows her paint and fabric options.

Notable: A human-size nutcracker named Nutty resides in Laurie's room. Nutty stays in the room during the first half of Day I, and because one homeowner feels that Nutty is staring at him, he paints over one of Nutty's eyes. Later, Nutty floats on a raft in a swimming pool. He makes a final appearance in the passenger seat of a golf cart driven by Amy Wynn.

Laurie's Room: ☺ ☺ ☹
Vern's Room: ☺ ☺ ☹

Maple Glen: Fiedler Road ✻

Cast: Paige, Laurie, Genevieve, Amy Wynn

The Rooms: Laurie paints the walls of a bedroom celadon green, creates a headboard from white and yellow silk squares, paints the existing furniture white, installs bamboo pieces as door hardware, and converts bamboo place mats into pillow shams. Using lilies as inspiration in a living room, Gen paints the walls a yellowed taupe, builds two new couches and a new coffee table, hangs large black and white family photos, and pins prints of vintage botanical postcards to the wall.

Attitude Check: Laurie repeatedly says she's "in a panic mode" about her room; Gen says she's in a "slo-mo hot zone," meaning that the high room temperature is making her zone out.

Laurie's Room: ☺ ☺ ☹
Gen's Room: ☺ ☺ ☹

Northampton: James Avenue ✻ 🔧

Cast: Paige, Hildi, Frank, Ty

The Rooms: Hildi updates a living room with mustard-gold paint, aubergine curtains, yellow and red tufted pillows, a sisal rug, sunflowers, and a river rock mosaic fireplace. Frank creates a nautical Nantucket theme in a living room by painting the walls pale sage, adding yellow and seafoam green pillows, wrapping rope around the coffee table legs to make the table resemble a pier, and building a dinghy-inspired dog bed.

Oops!: Hildi tries to use an industrial sander/scraper, but it won't turn to the right. Pandemonium breaks out as Hildi, Ty, and the male homeowner attempt to get the scraper to work correctly. Eventually, Ty runs it in left-hand circles while Hildi and the homeowner run around holding the cord to keep it from wrapping around Ty.

Amen: Frank and his homeowners say a prayer to the paint gods, thanking them for their color choice.

Quotable Quote: Frank: "OK, I'll work this in between my tennis match with the royal family and my tanning appointment."

Tool Time: Frank encourages his male homeowner to keep sewing, telling him to think of the machine as another power tool. The homeowner decides to think of it as a jigsaw.

Hildi's Room: ☺ ☺ ☹
Frank's Room: ☺ ☺ ☹

Providence: Phillips Street ✻

Cast: Paige, Hildi, Vern, Amy Wynn

The Rooms: Hildi adds sophistication to a living room by painting the walls slate gray, making butter yellow slipcovers, adding a touch of charcoal wax to an existing coffee table and side tables, and replacing the drop ceiling tiles with wood-tone panels. Vern uses the principles of feng shui in a living room by painting the walls and ceiling yellow for wealth, designing a coffee table that holds bamboo stalks for health, attaching small framed mirrors to the ceiling above a candle chandelier, and building a custom fish tank stand for the homeowner's large aquarium.

Lucky Vern: Vern removes the existing slipcover on the couch and discovers that the original upholstery color is cranberry, which perfectly matches his design.

Navel Alert!: Paige exposes her belly button for the first time while attaching Vern's mirrors to the ceiling.

Notable: Paige is nearly attacked by bees during the key swap.

Hildi's Room: ☺ ☺ ☹
Vern's Room: ☺ ☺ ☹

Providence: Wallis Avenue 💣💥 👶 🖌️

Cast: Paige, Genevieve, Frank, Amy Wynn

The Rooms: Gen brings a touch of Tuscany to a bedroom by painting the walls sage green, painting the ceiling yellow, installing floor-to-ceiling shelves, hanging ivy above the headboard, and using light and airy curtains and bed linens. Frank enlivens a kitchen by using several pastel shades of paint, creating a larger tabletop, laying a vinyl floor, and adding painted chevrons to the cabinets.

Notable: Frank uses his budget sparingly in order to buy the homeowners a dishwasher (they don't have one, and they have two kids). When Amy Wynn tells him that she can return two pieces of wood and enable him to buy the appliance, he does a touchdown victory dance.

Quotable Quote: Frank predicts the homeowners' reaction to the new dishwasher: "The squealing is gonna be like the Chicago stockyards when they see this."

Gen's Room: ☺ ☺ ☹
Frank's Room: ☺ ☺ ☹

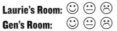

Boston: Ashfield Street ♥

Cast: Paige, Laurie, Genevieve, Ty

The Rooms: Laurie breathes new life into a kids' room by painting the walls lavender, creating a trundle bed, painting the existing furniture white, and using ribbons as accents. Gen adds a Moroccan touch to a kid's room by painting the walls and ceiling deep blue, installing a large curtained bed, hanging a Moroccan metal lamp, using gold fabric accents, and hanging white draperies.

Oops!: Paige drills through a plastic place mat to create a lampshade, but the bit comes out of the drill. When Gen tries to pull the bit out of the place mat, she finds that they've drilled through the homeowners' deck. A huge giggle fit ensues.

Happy Ending: The girls who live in Laurie's room like her design so much that they actually turn cartwheels.

Laurie's Room: ☺ ☺ ☹
Gen's Room: ☺ ☺ ☹

Springfield: Sunset Terrace 💣

Cast: Paige, Hildi, Vern, Ty

The Rooms: Hildi creates a Victorian look in a living room by painting the walls light putty, using blue and white print fabric for draperies and slipcovers, painting blue stripes on the wood floor, sewing a white faux-fur rug, and transforming the fireplace with a custom-built Victorian-style mantelpiece. Vern goes for an even more Victorian look in the other living room by painting the walls yellow, highlighting the homeowners' French provincial furniture, laying a Victorian rug, making a light fixture with silver mesh and hand-strung beads, and creating a custom art piece using celestial and fleur-de-lis stencils.

Notable: Hildi and Vern design against type in this episode, with mixed results.

Hildi's Room: ☺ ☺ ☹
Vern's Room: ☺ ☺ ☹

Boston: Institute Road

Cast: Paige, Doug, Frank, Ty

The Rooms: Doug looks to the leaves for inspiration in his "Autumnal Bliss" bedroom. He papers the walls with bark paper, upholsters the headboard in linen, hangs yellow linen draperies, and frames fall leaves as art. Frank creates a Shakespearean library by painting the walls red, hand-painting Elizabethan musician cutouts for the walls, and painting a rounded stone pattern on the floor.

Quotable Quote: Frank, on what may be under the carpet he's ripping up: "It could be the gates of heaven or the portals of hell."

Notable: Ty skeletons down the driveway on a wheeled ottoman multiple times, nearly crashing into piles of lumber.

Doug's Room: ☺ ☺ ☹
Frank's Room: ☺ ☺ ☹

Philadelphia: Jeannes Street

Cast: Paige, Genevieve, Vern, Amy Wynn

The Rooms: Gen turns a basement den into a 3-D *Scrabble* board by painting taupe and white grids on the floors and ceiling, installing a black wall-length bar, making pillows that mimic *Scrabble* board squares, and framing game boards to hang on the wall. Vern uses the holiday season for inspiration in a living room by painting the walls and ceiling deep red, making camel slipcovers and draperies, and building a dark wood armoire with mirrored doors.

Silly Gen!: Gen and Paige try to screw lazy Susan tops to bar stools. First, Gen's screws aren't long enough; then they can't get the screws in, and Gen realizes she has the drill in reverse; next their screws are too long, and the tops won't swivel. A huge giggle fit breaks out.

Time Test: Vern's male homeowner takes forever to wrap

---

lights around two mini pine trees.

Gen's Room: ☺ ☺ ☹
Vern's Room: ☺ ☺ ☹

New Jersey: Perth Road 🔌

Cast: Paige, Frank, Laurie, Amy Wynn

The Rooms: Frank gives a living room a homier feel by adding light camel paint, a coffee table topped with a picture frame, textured folk art on the wall, and a custom-built armoire ("It's kind of a puppet theater cathedral"). Laurie redoes a bedroom without altering the existing Queen Anne furniture. She paints the walls a warm apricot, builds a custom canopy that rests on top of the four-poster bed, and adds bookshelves as nightstands.

Say What?: Frank describes his design as a "formal, casual, yet funky over-the-top look."

Boys Club: Frank's male homeowner complains about having to sew, because he doesn't think it's a manly activity. However, he also points out that he's secure in his manhood. Frank retorts, "Well, then if you're so damned secure, start putting that stuffing in that pillow."

Quotable Quote: While cutting tree branches to use in his room, Frank says, "I have a college degree. Reduced to a beaver."

Fashion Report: Laurie straightens her hair for this episode.

Frank's Room: ☺ ☺ ☹
Laurie's Room: ☺ ☺ ☹

Maryland: Village Green

Cast: Paige, Genevieve, Doug, Amy Wynn

The Rooms: Gen refines a bedroom by painting one wall chocolate brown, covering the ceiling with gold metallic paint, installing a custom geometric shelving unit, making a fountain, decoupaging sewing patterns to a wall, and creating a light fixture out of a large wicker ball. Doug creates an elegant and sophisticated look in a bedroom by painting the walls gray, building a large upholstered headboard with storage in the back, painting the furniture white, and painting large Matisse-inspired figures directly on the wall.

Oops!: To create custom lampshades, Gen wraps rounded glass vases with plastic wrap and then winds glued string around them à la papier-mâché. Once the vases are dry, Gen and Paige put on safety glasses and start hammering the shades to break the vases on the inside. Gen thinks her idea of including the plastic wrap will keep them from having to touch any shards of glass. She's wrong. After a huge giggle fit, Gen looks into the camera and warns, "This project isn't for kids."

Name Game: Doug titles his room "Strip Stripe" for the gray and white striped fabric he uses to cover the headboard.

Gen's Room: ☺ ☺ ☹
Doug's Room: ☺ ☺ ☹

Maryland: Fairway Court

Cast: Paige, Vern, Doug, Amy Wynn

The Rooms: Vern softens a bedroom by painting the walls a soft gray, hanging charcoal draperies, suspending a canopy over the existing sleigh bed, and dangling 100 clear crystals from the canopy edge. Doug designs a fantasy bedroom suite for train enthusiasts by rounding the ceiling edges, covering the walls with blue paint and fabric, and building fake walls and windows to mimic the inside of a Pullman car.

Quotable Quote: Vern states during Designer Chat, "Precision doesn't have to go overtime; you just have to be well-planned."

Notable: Doug claims that this design is the biggest challenge he's taken on in a *Trading Spaces* episode. Paige refers to it as a "marvelous achievement."

Vern's Room: ☺ ☺ ☹
Doug's Room: ☺ ☺ ☹

Chicago: Edward Road 🔌

Cast: Paige, Frank, Laurie, Ty

The Rooms: Frank adds patina to a kitchen by using touches of terra-cotta, copper, and green paint. He also lays earth-tone vinyl flooring, paints a faux-tile backsplash, makes a large floorcloth, and adds a butcher-block island. Laurie gives a living room a touch of European flair by painting a faux-fresco finish in yellow tones, installing dark wooden beams on the ceiling, hanging burlap draperies, painting a faux-inlay top on an occasional table, and repeating an X motif throughout the room.

Quotable Quote: At the end of Day I Frank says, "I'm gonna go home, have a pedicure, manicure, shower, have my designer stylist come in and...I'll see you in the morning."

Laurie's Design Theory: "I want to give them a room that is a basic skeleton with beautiful walls...and then, hopefully, what I trigger them to do is get a new love seat."

Frank's Room: ☺ ☺ ☹
Laurie's Room: ☺ ☺ ☹

Chicago: Spaulding Avenue 😮

Cast: Paige, Doug, Hildi, Ty

The Rooms: Doug adds a little funk to a living room by painting the walls yellow, using Venetian plaster to make black and yellow blocks on a wall, upholstering the furniture with zebra-print fabric, and suspending a tabletop from the ceiling to create a dining area. Hildi brings the outdoors into a bedroom. She paints the walls cream and the trim deep plum and then draws large "swooshes" of grass on the walls with pastels. She adds a row of grass planter boxes along one wall, uses bursts of orange in pillows, and installs a large wooden bed.

Conflict: Doug wants to glaze a 2-inch border around the wood floor. He paints a small strip to show what it will look like, and the homeowners argue against it. He wipes it off with a pouty face.

Sticky Situation: After drawing grass blades on the wall, Hildi and her homeowners seal the chalk pastel with several cans of hair spray.

Oops!: Ty can't get the window bench into the bedroom. He eventually has to remove the center legs to get it inside the bedroom door.

Doug's Room: ☺ ☺ ☹
Hildi's Room: ☺ ☺ ☹

163

Chicago: Fairview Avenue

Cast: Paige, Vern, Genevieve, Ty

The Rooms: Vern brightens a kitchen by painting the walls pear green, painting the cabinets white, creating a new cabinet for storage, making a new table, laying a black and white geometric rug, upholstering a storage bench that doubles as seating at the table, and hanging upholstered cushions against the wall above the bench. Gen gives the lodge look to a basement living room by painting the walls cinnamon, installing a pine plank ceiling, hanging wood wainscoting, slipcovering the furniture, and highlighting the fireplace with built-in shelves.

Oops!: Gen breaks the heel of her boot and goes to Ty for the repair.

Rest Time: Ty tries to take a break on a school bus, and Gen has to drag him back to work.

Vern's Room: ☺ ☺ ☹
Gen's Room: ☺ ☺ ☹

Colorado: Berry Avenue ❓ ☹

Cast: Paige, Genevieve, Hildi, Amy Wynn

The Rooms: Gen paints the walls of a kitchen bright eggplant, paints the cabinets vanilla-sage, removes the center panels of the cabinet doors to showcase the dishes inside, and prints each family member's face on a chair cover for personalized seating. Hildi creates an intimate living room by painting the walls a deep chocolate brown, using sage fabrics, transforming the coffee table into a large ottoman, and installing a wall-size fountain made to mimic the existing windows.

Yucky Moment: Gen explains her color choices by tearing apart a boiled artichoke. Paige pops the bitter heart into her mouth and nearly gags.

Resourceful: Gen sketches her table design—including measurements—on Amy Wynn's palm.

Joke Time: Gen's homeowners rent a jackhammer and use it in a bucket of hardened concrete to make their neighbors think their floor is being ripped out.

Technical Stuff: Gen attempts to explain how she uses her laptop to reproduce the family photos for the chair covers. Gen describes the computer program she's using as a "special program for a special girl."

Silly Stuff: During Designer Chat, Paige and Gen wear the chair covers with the homeowners' faces over their heads and role-play the homeowners' reaction to their new room.

What Was She Thinking?: Hildi and Paige cover the bottom of a plastic window box planter with silicone to seal it. When they try to set a large piece of glass in the box to create the fountain, Paige cuts through the silicone, breaking the seal. Water quickly seeps across the wood floor.

Gen's Room: ☺ ☺ ☹
Hildi's Room: ☺ ☺ ☹

Colorado: Cherry Street ❓👀

Cast: Paige, Genevieve, Laurie, Amy Wynn

The Rooms: Gen gives a living room a punch of personality by painting the walls brick red with sage accents, hanging antlers on the walls, installing floor-to-ceiling shelving, making a focal point out of one of the homeowners' landscape photos, and creating an inlaid rug. Laurie applies a touch of mod to a living room by painting gray and yellow horizontal stripes on the walls, building a new glass-top coffee table, hanging silver silk draperies, and adding a piece of custom artwork.

Quotable Quote: Gen describes the original look of her room by saying, "If this were a country, it would be Beigeland."

What Was She Thinking?: Rather than lay a green rug on top of the beige carpet, Gen cuts out a patch of the carpet and lays the new rug inside. Gen warns viewers, "Don't do this if you're renting."

Gen's Room: ☺ ☺ ☹
Laurie's Room: ☺ ☺ ☹

Colorado: Andes Way 🔌

Cast: Paige, Frank, Vern, Amy Wynn

The Rooms: Frank creates a family-friendly living room by rag-rolling the walls with cream and peach paint, hanging valances coated with brown builder's paper, building a white and sage armoire, and creating a kids' nook with a large art table, plant murals on the walls, and wooden clouds nailed to the ceiling. Vern stripes a living room, laying two colors of laminate flooring in alternating stripes, painting a red horizontal stripe on the khaki walls, and continuing the same stripe across the draperies.

Say What?: Describing his paint technique, Frank says, "It's kinda, like, goth-eyed wonky."

Notable: When Amy Wynn gives up on helping out with one of Frank's crafts project, he calls her a "craft wimp."

Frank's Room: ☺ ☺ ☹
Vern's Room: ☺ ☺ ☹

Colorado: Stoneflower Drive 🧨👶✳

Cast: Paige, Frank, Doug, Amy Wynn

The Rooms: Frank injects some whimsy into a bedroom by painting the walls celadon green, building a large headboard that mimics a skyline, creating a matching dog bed, and hanging gold curtains. Doug updates a living room with a design he calls "Smoke Screen." He paints the walls moss green, adds pewter accents, hangs pleated metal screening, and builds screen doors to cover fireplace shelving.

Gotcha!: Frank brings in tacky dolphin pillows, and the homeowner says that she loves them. Frank laughs and explains that he's only using them as inexpensive pillow forms.

Helping Out: Doug lounges in a deck chair drinking iced tea while reading faux-finish directions to his homeowners. He tosses them supplies instead of getting up.

Wise Words: Frank, during Designer Chat: "I wanted to give them a room that has, like most relationships or marriages, some whimsy, some peacefulness, and a little bit of tactile sensitivity and sexuality."

Frank's Room: ☺ ☺ ☹
Doug's Room: ☺ ☺ ☹

Seattle: 137th Street 👶☹♥

Cast: Paige, Doug, Frank, Ty

The Rooms: Doug does "Denim Deluxe" in a living room. He paints a white grid pattern on chocolate walls, slipcovers the furniture with brown and ivory denim, makes art pieces with brightly colored tissue paper, lowers the existing coffee table, installs white wainscoting, and builds a white facade to cover the brick fireplace. Frank brightens a living room by painting the walls reddish orange and yellow, installing a new mantel, hanging shelves on either side of the fireplace, making a fireplace screen painted with folk art characters, and creating a window valance with place mats and clothespins.

Conflict: Homeowner dissension abounds in this classic episode! The living room homeowners leave Doug strict instructions not to paint their fireplace, but of course, Doug wants to paint it white. His homeowners repeatedly argue with him about it. When Doug states that he's not happy, one of his homeowners turns ultrapositive and says, "It's OK not to be happy sometimes!" When Doug leaves the room in a huff, she looks to the camera and says, "Well, now he's a little cranky."

Resourceful?: While Doug pouts, Ty problem-solves by designing a facade to "slipcover" the brick. As he and Ty are installing the facade, Doug prophetically says, "This may be my shining moment."

Nasty Side: While working with Paige and his homeowners to make the tissue paper art, Doug places a wooden Santa figure on the table and says that he brought Frank along to oversee their crafting.

Huh?: Frank describes what he wants to paint on the walls by saying, "We're going to be doing a kind of rectangular, kind of checky, not really country, not really contemporary, just homey, cottagey, but with a kind of a more upbeat level."

Reveal-ing Moments: A classic Reveal that must be seen to be believed! The denim living room homeowners are extremely disappointed with their room (the male homeowner surmises Doug's design as "I see a lot of firewood"), and the female homeowner leaves the room in tears while her microphone continues running.

Doug's Room: ☺ ☺ ☹
Frank's Room: ☺ ☺ ☹

Seattle: Dakota Street 🔌

Cast: Paige, Vern, Laurie, Ty

The Rooms: Vern adds drama and romance to a living room by painting the walls golden yellow, hanging brown draperies, building an armoire with red upholstered door panels, slipcovering the furniture in white fabric dyed with

tea bags, and constructing red candle torchères. Laurie tries to convince her homeowners that she can warm up a bedroom with parchment-color paint, soft white and blue fabrics, various chocolate brown accents on the furniture and headboard, and painted partition screens.

Guy Thing: Vern's male homeowner sits down at the sewing machine and is confused about how to make it "go."

Yucky Moment: Paige catches a large fish while standing in a fish market during the introduction.

Reveal-ing Moment: Both of the female homeowners dislike their rooms. In fact, the bedroom homeowner hates her room and keeps talking about all the work she'll have to do the next day to change it.

Vern's Room: ☺ ☺ ☹
Laurie's Room: ☺ ☺ ☹

Seattle: 56th Place ☹ 💲 ❓

Cast: Paige, Hildi, Genevieve, Ty

The Rooms: Hildi covers a basement rec room in magenta and taupe fabric hung from the ceiling. She also builds new coffee and side tables and slipcovers new sofas with magenta fabric. Gen creates an Asian living room, using shimmery silver and red paints and coating one wall in a metal paint that oxidizes to a rusted finish. She makes a valance out of an obi and uses cedar flowerpots as picture frames.

Oops!: While Gen and Paige are crafting a lamp, they recount all of the bad things that have happened when they work on projects together. While lamenting all the things they've broken, Paige slips with the glass globe she's cleaning and breaks it. Gen states, "This is a show of human errors."

Notable: Hildi surprises her homeowners by spray-painting the existing upholstered furniture magenta. Later, one of Hildi's homeowners brings Paige in with her eyes closed and then reveals the painted furniture. Paige is shocked and says that it looks bad.

Budget Crisis: Hildi arrives on Day 2 to find that the tarp blew off the freshly painted furniture; the furniture has been rained on and ruined. Paige eventually agrees to break the rules, letting Hildi go severely over budget in order to buy new furniture. Hildi leaves, and returns with two new sofas (total cost: $500) that are eventually slipcovered.

Hildi's Room: ☺ ☺ ☹
Gen's Room: ☺ ☺ ☹

Oregon: Alyssum Avenue 🔌 ❓ 🔨

Cast: Paige, Hildi, Genevieve, Amy Wynn

The Rooms: Hildi cozies a bedroom by upholstering the walls and ceiling with silver-blue fabric, building a bed from storage cubes, draping sheer white fabric from the ceiling center over the bed corners, hanging a chandelier above the bed, and adding a blue monogram to white bed linens. Gen adds a graphic touch to a living room by painting the walls bright yellow, covering a wall with 6-inch squares, building cedar shelving under the stairs, and hanging clotheslines to display art and photos.

Never-Ending Project: Gen's wall of squares requires a ridiculous number of steps. The design calls for more than a thousand squares of wood; each square has to be stacked on top of others to create different heights; and the stacked squares must be glued together, stapled to reinforce the glue, primed, painted, hung on the wall, and puttied over to cover the nail holes.

Hildi's Room: ☺ ☺ ☹
Gen's Room: ☺ ☺ ☹

Oregon: Alsea Court 🔌 🧨 💲

Cast: Paige, Frank, Laurie, Amy Wynn

The Rooms: Frank goes south of the border in a kitchen by painting a serape on the ceiling, making a basket-weave wall treatment with sheet metal strips, painting the cabinet door center panels silver, designing a distressed tabletop, and upholstering dining chairs with serape fabric. Laurie brings warmth to a living room by painting the walls amber, using several expensive fabrics in warm harvest shades, building a long armoire with gold filigree door insets, and designing a large central ottoman.

Quotable Quotes: Frank again: "I feel very Carmen Miranda-ish. Now, quick, get me a pineapple drink and a funny hat."

Frank's Room: ☺ 😐 ☹
Laurie's Room: ☺ 😐 ☹

Portland: Everett Street 👶 ☹

Cast: Paige, Doug, Vern, Amy Wynn

The Rooms: Doug transforms a family room into an Art Deco theater by painting the floors and ceiling chocolate brown, covering the walls with chocolate brown fabric, building graduated platforms for silver chairs, suspending the television from the ceiling, and installing aisle lights. Vern creates a cohesive look in a living/dining room by painting the walls sage green and hanging sage draperies with white satin stripes on the windows and the walls of the dining area. He also builds a custom armoire and buffet with square wooden insets stained various colors and creates a custom lampshade with handmade art paper.

Fashion Report: Doug wears a knit skullcap; Vern's hair is especially spiky.

Conflict: Doug's homeowners continually question whether there will be room for a computer in the finished design. By the morning of Day 2, Doug is weary of fending them off and mixes a glass of antacid.

Guy Thing: Vern explains stuffing a pillow and mounting a wall sconce to his male homeowner by relating these processes to taxidermy, the homeowner's hobby.

Doug's Room: ☺ 😐 ☹
Vern's Room: ☺ 😐 ☹

Santa Clara: Lafayette Street ⊸⫿▮

Cast: Paige, Frank, Laurie, Ty

The Rooms: Frank adds a festive touch to the living room of a Delta Gamma residence by painting the walls two shades of a peachy orange; highlighting the curved ceiling with stenciled stars, triangles, swirls, and dots; painting the sorority letters above the fireplace; and installing a window bench seat. Laurie updates the Delta Gamma chapter room by painting the walls a muted seafoam, stenciling yellow anchors on the walls, designing a coffee table with hidden additional seating, and making a candelabra out of a captain's wheel.

Paint Fun: Frank reveals the wall colors by having both the sorority sisters close their eyes, dip their hands in the paint, and then smear it on the wall.

Notable: Frank does a cartwheel during the sped-up footage of his team removing furniture from his room.

Go, Girl: Laurie reminisces about her sorority days as a Kappa and talks about having to dress up like Carmen Miranda and sing "Kappa, Kappa-cabana" to the tune of Barry Manilow's "Copacabana."

Acting!: Paige pretends to be a surprised sorority sister at the last Reveal and starts screaming and hugging the sorority members.

Budget Crunch: Over budget by 11 cents, Laurie presents Paige with that amount during Designer Chat.

Frank's Room: ☺ 😐 ☹
Laurie's Room: ☺ 😐 ☹

California: Corte Rosa ☹

Cast: Paige, Vern, Laurie, Ty

The Rooms: Vern gives a bedroom an exotic resort decor by painting the walls light chino, upholstering the bedside tabletops with faux leather, adding tribal- and safari-print

fabrics to the draperies and bed linens, hanging a red glass light fixture, and building storage cabinets on a large plant ledge. Laurie creates romance in a bedroom by painting the walls sage green, hanging a French tester canopy above the bed, painting the existing furniture mocha brown, installing a window seat with storage cabinets, and hanging dark green draperies.

For Fun: Vern, Laurie, and Ty pedal tiny three-wheeled bikes at the start of the show.

Quotable Quote: Commenting on the romance of his room, Vern says to Paige during his Designer Chat, "If this doesn't produce a third child, this is gonna be a total failure."

Vern's Room: ☺ 😐 ☹
Laurie's Room: ☺ 😐 ☹

California: Grenadine Way $ ✳

Cast: Paige, Vern, Frank, Ty

The Rooms: Vern looks to vintage Indian fabrics for inspiration in a bedroom. He paints the walls soft blue, lays wood laminate flooring, installs a large headboard of basket-woven iridescent fabric, and hangs amber glass candleholders. Frank gives ethnic flair to a living room by painting a mantel with lines of mustard, white, taupe, and black, designing a large wooden sculpture, and building a new coffee table, armoire, and valance.

Get Well!: Vern has laryngitis this episode and is often barely able to speak. He tells Ty on Day 1 that he's doing his best Darth Vader impersonation. By the morning of Day 2, he has to communicate with his homeowners by writing on pieces of paper.

Quotable Quote: Frank describes for Paige how he feels about staying under budget, saying simply, "I'm puffed."

Notable: Penny-wise Vern is over budget (!) by $2.47.

Vern's Room: ☺ 😐 ☹
Frank's Room: ☺ 😐 ☹

Berkeley: Prospect Street
$ 🔌 👶 ♥

Cast: Paige, Doug, Genevieve, Ty

The Rooms: Doug cleans up the Delta Upsilon fraternity chapter room (and goes "DU-clectic") by painting the walls lime green, installing bench seating, constructing two huge circular ottomans upholstered with lime and orange fabrics, and suspending a tabletop from the ceiling. Gen adds classic Hollywood-style glamour to the Alpha Omicron Pi sorority chapter room by painting white and silver stripes on the walls, adding black and silver throw pillows, building a large armoire, and commissioning her team to trace silhouettes of Paige and herself for wall art.

Fashion Report: Doug dons leather pants (and a crisp blue oxford shirt, of course). Paige sports black, horn-rimmed glasses at the start of the show.

Yucky Moments: Doug is amazed by how filthy his assigned room is. When it's time to clear the room, Doug starts pitching everything out the third-story window—including the sofa. Later, he has his team put on biohazard gear to sweep and clean the room before they start redecorating.

Huh?: Gen tells her eager team members that she wants to create "a couch that screams 'Sexy, sexy, sexy!'"

Diva Fit Details: When Doug points out that one of his team members missed a spot while painting, she paints his shirt. A full-fledged paint fight ensues.

Conflict: Doug's team fights to keep the existing beer lights in the room, rejecting the custom lights Doug wants to make. Doug eventually gives in.

Doug's Room: ☺ 😐 ☹
Gen's Room: ☺ 😐 ☹

Oakland: Webster Street
☹ 💣 ❓ ♥

Cast: Paige, Hildi, Genevieve, Amy Wynn

The Rooms: Hildi experiments in a living room by covering the walls with straw. She also installs a wall of bookshelves, covers the fireplace with copper mesh and glass rods, and screens the windows with wooden louvered blinds. Gen brightens a kitchen by painting the cabinets yellow and the walls cobalt blue, building a tile-top island and kids' table, personalizing dishware with family art and photos, and designing a backlit display shelf for a glass bottle collection.

The Last Straw: Hildi's wall treatment turns out to be high-maintenance. She and her homeowners spend much time brushing off straw that didn't adhere and hand-trimming long pieces.

Quotable Quote: Hildi is truly amazed when one of her homeowners explains that the kids who will live in the room may tear straw off the walls and eat it. Hildi questions the homeowner's concern by asking, "Do they eat lint off of the sofa?" The homeowner tells her the children do. Hildi then asks, "Do they walk around outside and eat grass?" The homeowner tells her they do indeed.

Fashion Report: Gen has her hair wrapped in numerous tight little buns à la Scary Spice. One of her homeowners uses a hair bun as a pincushion while sewing. Gen lets her hair down for her Designer Chat, to voluminous effect.

Reveal-ing Moments: The living room homeowners seem to like the design but are unsure about having straw on the walls with two young children in the household. When they demonstrate how the kids will pick at the straw, Paige eats two small pieces of straw.

Hildi's Room: ☺ 😐 ☹
Gen's Room: ☺ 😐 ☹

California: Peralta Street ❓ ♥

Cast: Paige, Hildi, Doug, Amy Wynn

The Rooms: Hildi divides a living room into quadrants by painting two opposite corners of the room and ceiling silver and painting the remaining corners and ceiling space violet. She supplements the look with a clear-glass mosaic on the fireplace surround, four metal chairs, and a large circular ottoman upholstered in silver and violet. Doug thinks pink in a dining room. He paints the walls bubble gum pink, paints the ceiling chocolate brown, upholsters new dining chairs with lime green T-shirts, and tops new storage units with green gazing balls.

Musical Moments: In this tuneful episode, the four homeowners play together in their band as Doug and Hildi dance at the start of the show. Later, Doug attempts to rap, and Hildi plays guitar badly while assigning homework to her team.

Oops!: Hildi attempts to drill through four large stones so she can attach them as legs on her ottoman. That doesn't work, so she has to use an adhesive to connect them.

Yucky Moment: Hildi photocopies parts of her own body to make wall art.

Nasty Side: Doug throws all the homeowners' knickknacks into the trash at the start of the show.

Hildi's Room: ☺ 😐 ☹
Doug's Room: ☺ 😐 ☹

Los Angeles: Willoughby Avenue ☹ 🔌

Cast: Paige, Doug, Genevieve, Ty

The Rooms: Doug sees red in a living room: He stencils the walls and doors in red and white, using a rectangular graphic based on a pillow pattern. He paints the ceiling gray, lays a red shag rug, and builds a U-shape couch with red upholstery. Gen designs a swingin' living room with 1950s flair by painting the walls aqua, covering floor stains with black paint, transforming mod place mats into wall sconces, slipcovering a futon in white vinyl, and laying a bookcase on its side to create a new coffee table.

Fashion Report: Gen wears a Britney Spears-inspired tube sock on her arm. Doug's leather pants make another appearance, and he appears to be growing a goatee.

Safety First!: When Paige and Gen go to a local flower market to buy orchids late on Day 2, Gen runs across the street without looking both ways.

Flaming Success: Gen lights a cigar with a blowtorch when her room comes together.

Gen's Design Theory: "I think it's important whenever you do something that's remotely hip...that you are able to update. Otherwise you're stuck in something that becomes very passé."

Reveal-ing Moments: Both male homeowners swear during The Reveals and have to be bleeped.

Quotable Quote: During the end credits, Doug's male homeowner does a fine Paige impression, saying, "Hi, America. I'm Paige Davis. Look at my cute little Sandy Duncan hair."

Doug's Room: ☺ ☹ ☹
Gen's Room: ☺ ☹ ☹

Los Angeles: Springdale Drive 💣

Cast: Paige, Vern, Laurie, Ty

The Rooms: Vern brightens a dining room by painting the walls yellow, hanging bronze draperies, installing a wall-length buffet with built-in storage, and designing a multi-armed halogen chandelier with gold vellum shades and a hanging candleholder. Laurie enlivens a basement den by painting the walls yellow, slipcovering the existing furniture with natural cotton duck fabric, sewing an aqua Roman shade, installing several yellow and aqua shadow box shelves, designing a folding screen to mask exercise equipment, and painting squares and rectangles in various shades of aqua to create custom wall art.

Oops!: Vern's homeowners write positive thoughts on the walls in pencil, with the intent of painting over them as they work on the room. The writing shows through the paint, and they have to go back and clean off what they wrote.

Guy Thing: Vern and Ty have trouble bringing in the buffet. It's too long to make several of the turns in the house, and they bump the corner of it on a doorway, scuffing the piece.

Vern's Room: ☺ ☹ ☹
Laurie's Room: ☺ ☹ ☹

California: Abbeywood Lane 💣

Cast: Paige, Frank, Hildi, Ty

The Rooms: Frank gives a living room a cohesive look by painting the walls sage green; building an upholstered wall hanging in shades of peach, coral, and yellow; painting a life-size image of the homeowners' toddler on the wall; making throw pillows out of fabric designed by the homeowner; and crafting candleholders out of 4×4s covered with license plates. Hildi creates her version of a nautical living room by painting the walls black; nailing lightly stained 1×2s on the walls in a vertical arrangement; building two large couches; using seafoam fabric to upholster the couch, create throw pillows, and make draperies; and mounting photos of the ocean onto blocks of wood.

Oops!: Ty demolishes the existing pass-through in Frank's room and takes a chunk of the wall with it.

Notable: Paige and Frank "kiss" while wearing dust masks.

Frank's Room: ☺ ☹ ☹
Hildi's Room: ☺ ☹ ☹

Austin: La Costa Drive (celebrity episode)

Cast: Paige, Vern, Hildi, Ty

The Rooms: In the first celebrity episode of *Trading Spaces*, Vern breathes life into the bonus room of Dixie Chicks lead vocalist Natalie Maines. Vern paints the walls yellow, installs a wall-length desk and sewing unit, hangs a huge chandelier, and sews throw pillows, draperies, and bed linens with shimmery red fabric. Hildi adds style to a sewing room, which belongs to Natalie's mother, by railroading gray and sage fabric on the walls, installing wooden louvered wall dividers, building a 14-foot couch, reupholstering a vintage shampoo chair, and covering a coffee table with slate tiles.

Call-In: Ty is too busy to come over to Vern's room during Day I, so Vern phones in his measurements to him.

Quick Chick: Hildi and Natalie have a sewing race while working on the couch bolsters. Natalie wins.

Vern's Room: ☺ ☹ ☹
Hildi's Room: ☺ ☹ ☹

Texas: Sherwood Street 💣 🔌

Cast: Paige, Frank, Genevieve, Amy Wynn

The Rooms: Frank transforms a kitchen by removing strawberry wallpaper, sponge-painting a focal point wall, hanging new draperies with a pear motif, painting the avocado green floor and countertops with faux tiles, and hanging a thin plywood sunburst around the existing fluorescent light. Gen conjures a New England cottage feel in a bedroom by painting three of the walls pale smoke, painting one of the walls ultrabright white, building a fireplace mantel-style headboard, creating curtain tiebacks from red neckties, sewing bed pillows from pinstriped suit jackets, distressing the existing ceiling fan, and adding a library nook.

Quotable Quote: Frank calms his homeowners' fears of a new painting technique by saying, "I will take you by the hand, lead you to the river of paint, dip you in it, and baptize you to the great religion of faux finishes."

Resourceful: Near the end of Day 2, Gen pulls in a stone bench from the garden because she can't afford to buy one.

Reveal-ing Moments: The kitchen homeowners love their room so much they won't stop screeching. Paige eventually puts her fingers in her ears.

Frank's Room: ☺ ☹ ☹
Gen's Room: ☺ ☹ ☹

Houston: Sawdust Street

❓ ✳ 💲 ♥

Cast: Paige, Laurie, Doug, Amy Wynn

The Rooms: Laurie refines a living room by painting the walls margarine yellow, building a wall-length bookshelf, hanging bamboo blinds and yellow drapery panels, and adding two spicy orange chairs. Doug goes "Zen/Goth" in a living room by painting the walls blood red, building an L-shape couch, hanging a large wrought-iron light fixture, and blowing up a photo of the female homeowner in lingerie and knee-high boots to hang over the fireplace.

Notable: Laurie announces that she is pregnant.

Oops!: Laurie's homeowners do such a bad job painting the bookshelf that Laurie has them scrape off the paint and redo it.

Sketchy: Doug draws his couch design for Amy Wynn on a toy magnetic drawing board.

Resourceful: Doug steals a pool noodle (to stuff his couch's bolster) from a kid playing in a pool. The kid chases after him, yelling, "Give me back my noodle!"

Yucky Moment: Doug finds the revealing photo to hang over the fireplace by digging through the female homeowner's drawers.

Laurie's Room: ☺ ☹ ☹
Doug's Room: ☺ ☹ ☹

Houston: Appalachian Trail 💣 ✳

Cast: Paige, Doug, Laurie, Amy Wynn

The Rooms: Laurie adds style to an office/playroom by painting the walls terra-cotta, building a large shelving and desk unit with plumbing conduit, painting the existing coffee table and armoire in eggshell and black, adding new seating, and creating the illusion of symmetry with cream draperies on an off-center window. Doug goes for a soft look in a bedroom by painting the walls pale blue, upholstering a tall headboard in blue chenille, sewing new blue and white bed linens, and installing custom light fixtures.

Fashion Report: Doug appears to suddenly have a fair amount of gray hair.

Name Game: Doug titles his room "A Pretty Room *by Doug*" (and yes, the italics are important).

Cheer Up!: Doug's female homeowner is a cheerleading coach. Her squad appears in the driveway and does a cheer for Doug: "Fix that space. You're an ace. Go, Doug, Go. You're a pro." Perhaps inspired by the cheerleading, Doug does a cartwheel later in the show.

Doug's Room: ☺ ☹ ☹
Laurie's Room: ☺ ☹ ☹

Plano: Bent Horn Court ☹

Cast: Paige, Genevieve, Vern, Ty

The Rooms: Gen regresses as she designs a playroom, painting multicolor polka dots on the walls, cutting movable circles of outdoor carpeting for the floors, building a large castle-shape puppet theater, hanging fabric-covered tire swings, and designing four upholstered squares on wheels, with storage space inside. Vern gets in touch with his rustic side in a living room by laying natural-color adhesive carpet tiles, painting an existing armoire and other furniture pieces black, and building a combination ottoman/coffee table/bench unit.

Go, Girl: Gen sends Paige on a mission around the house to find objects with different textures that Gen can frame and hang as kid-friendly art.

Gen's Room: ☺ ☹ ☹
Vern's Room: ☺ ☹ ☹

Plano: Shady Valley Road 🙀

Cast: Paige, Hildi, Doug, Ty

The Rooms: Hildi creates a two-tone bedroom by painting the walls bright white, installing 12-inch orange baseboards, building a new head- and footboard that match the pitch of the cathedral ceiling and covering them with white slipcovers, and upholstering a chair with white faux fur. Doug adds sophisticated style to a playroom by painting the wall moss green ("Moss Madness"), installing beams on the ceiling in a barnlike formation, building a basket-weave armoire, revamping a futon into a daybed, and hanging bifold doors on a toy closet.

Gifted: The two female homeowners are budding interior designers and have a business making accessories. They present Paige with a small lamp during the key swap.

Conflict: Hildi plans to dye the carpet in her room orange, but her female homeowner is adamantly opposed to the idea. They have several discussions about dyeing the carpet, with the homeowner becoming increasingly forceful in her opposition. At one point, Hildi asks rhetorically why she's been asked to design the room if she's not going to be allowed to follow through on her vision, noting, "Everyone in America knows I can rip up that carpet if I want to." Hildi compromises by sprinkling orange flower petals across the carpet for the Reveal.)

Hildi's Room: ☺ ☹ ☹
Doug's Room: ☺ ☹ ☹

Texas: Sutton Court 💲

Cast: Paige, Laurie, Frank, Ty

The Rooms: Laurie designs a kitchen, using the homeowners' china for inspiration. She paints the walls taupe with white trim, builds large wooden shadow boxes to display china pieces, hangs new light fixtures, and uses taupe fabric for the window treatments and chair cushions. Frank works with a Southwest theme in a living room, adding chamois-cloth accents to the existing furniture, building a footstool out of a saddle, hanging several custom-made art pieces, designing a Mission-style armoire, and making potted cactus out of vegetables.

Notable: Frank is hoarse throughout the episode and tells Paige, "I sound bad, but I am so perky."

Laurie's Room: ☺ 😐 ☹
Frank's Room: ☺ 😐 ☹

Raleigh: Legging Lane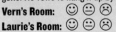

Cast: Paige, Frank, Hildi, Amy Wynn

The Rooms: Hildi adds romance to a bedroom by painting the walls slate gray, hanging smoky plum draperies, sewing a tufted lavender coverlet, framing a favorite picture of the Eiffel Tower, and building cubic bench seats and nightstands. Frank lets his creativity flow in a playroom by painting walls, furniture, doors, and floors in a multitude of pastel colors. He also hides a large refrigerator, builds an armoire to house media equipment, and designs a large toy chest.

Oops!: When Paige brings the homeowners into Hildi's room for the Reveal, she accidentally leads the male homeowner into the TV stand, banging his leg.

Paint Explosion!: Frank uses paint in every shade of the rainbow—and then some.

Frank's Room: ☺ 😐 ☹
Hildi's Room: ☺ 😐 ☹

North Carolina: Southerby Drive ✳

Cast: Paige, Doug, Hildi, Amy Wynn

The Rooms: Doug adds an Eastern touch to a bedroom by painting the walls china blue and painting white chinoiserie murals. He builds a black four-poster bed with PVC pipe, adds a custom-built sculpture, hangs white draperies, and paints the furniture black. Hildi also displays Eastern influences in a bedroom, painting the walls a soft green and installing a wall of shoji screens to create a headboard. She covers the screens and the existing furniture with lavender crackle finish, hangs lavender draperies, and upholsters with purple fabric.

Quotable Quote: Hildi's female homeowner says to her while upholstering, "Why did I ever doubt you, Hildi?"

Doug's Room: ☺ 😐 ☹
Hildi's Room: ☺ 😐 ☹

Wake Forest: Rodney Bay ✳

Cast: Paige, Vern, Laurie, Amy Wynn

The Rooms: Vern adds drama to a bedroom by painting the walls gray, attaching a fabric canopy to the ceiling, designing a headboard with interior lights that shine out of the top, painting the existing furniture black, and upholstering a chair with gray flannel. Laurie brightens a living room by painting the walls a bold shade of green, installing two floor-to-ceiling shelving units with crown molding, hanging yellow draperies, adding several pillows in warm harvest shades to the existing off-white sofa, and hanging a new parchment-shade light fixture.

Quotable Quote: In order to convince her homeowners that she must remove the existing ceiling fan, Laurie states, "I cannot in good faith do this room and not do this."

Reveal-ing Moments: Both sets of homeowners love their rooms, but the male living room homeowner swears twice upon opening his eyes and finding that the ceiling fan is gone. He vows to hang it up by the next morning.

Vern's Room: ☺ 😐 ☹
Laurie's Room: ☺ 😐 ☹

Season 3

Maine: George Road ⑦ 💣

Cast: Paige, Doug, Genevieve, Ty

The Rooms: Doug adds warmth to a kitchen by painting the walls umber, painting the woodwork white, installing a butcher-block countertop, building a large pantry unit with bifold doors, and sewing a large tablecloth. Gen updates a dark kitchen by painting the walls bright green, installing a black and white tile countertop, building a butcher-block island, hanging wood laminate wall paneling, and installing a 1930s light fixture.

Quotable Quotes: Doug's female homeowner tells her husband that Doug is "easy on the eyes." She goes on to say, "He hasn't been a real jerk yet."

Yucky Moments: Doug, Ty, and Paige make several laxative and lubricant jokes because the new countertop has to be rubbed with mineral oil.

Girl Power: When Gen's male homeowner gets a bit too excited about working with a pretty young woman, Gen takes control of the situation, telling him, "If I can handle power tools, I can handle you."

Budget Boasting: When Gen learns her budget is at $776.52, she looks into the camera and says, "Beat that, Doug!"

Doug's Room: ☺ 😐 ☹
Gen's Room: ☺ 😐 ☹

Portland: Rosemont Avenue ✳

Cast: Paige, Laurie, Vern, Ty

The Rooms: Laurie goes nautical in a living room by painting the walls deep aqua blue, painting the fireplace white, putting a cream-tone paint wash on wooden chairs and upholstering them with zebra-print fabric, and installing a vintage mercury glass chandelier. Vern brightens a living room by painting the walls yellow, hanging black and yellow Roman shades, installing French doors, covering the ceiling with white steel squares, hanging a ceiling fan, using black slipcovers for the existing furniture, and adding silver fold-up trays to serve as side tables and a coffee table.

Design Insight: Laurie says this is the first time that her paint color choice on *Trading Spaces* was not inspired by fabric. (Her inspiration in this case was the name of the paint color, which refers to the bay where the episode was filmed.)

Notable: Vern actually installs an all-white ceiling fan in his room! He points out that it's a *Trading Spaces* first.

Laurie's Room: ☺ 😐 ☹
Vern's Room: ☺ 😐 ☹

Maine: Joseph Drive 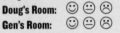 👶 ⑦

Cast: Paige, Laurie, Frank, Ty

The Rooms: Laurie enlivens a bedroom by painting the walls soft yellow, building an Asian-style shelving unit, designing a new headboard, sewing gray and white toile bedding, and adding an unusual floral light fixture. Frank shows another side of his design style in a bachelor's bedroom. He paints the walls and ceiling dark blue-green, hangs simple white draperies, sews a large plastic envelope to hold a pencil drawing of a leaf on the wall, builds a table that houses three wooden bins, and jazzes up a rocking chair with pet collars.

Notable: This is Laurie's last show before having her baby.

Quotable Quote: Frank, on his room design: "I want this to be the pit of wild monkey love."

Really?: Frank repeatedly tells anyone who will listen that this room will not contain any faux finishes or distressed objects. When Paige challenges him and says that he'll paint a chicken somewhere, he claims that he's only painted a chicken once in the history of *Trading Spaces*.

Laugh Riot: Frank and one of his homeowners make custom candleholders with metal pipe nipples and flanges. The homeowner becomes giggly at the mention of pipe nipples, and she and Frank can't stop laughing throughout the project.

Yucky Moment: Frank straps pet collars on an existing rocking chair, explaining coyly that they can function as arm and leg restraints for visitors to the bachelor pad.

Laurie's Room: ☺ 😐 ☹
Frank's Room: ☺ 😐 ☹

Long Island: Steuben Boulevard 🔌 ☹

Cast: Paige, Edward, Frank, Ty

The Rooms: Edward jazzes up a bedroom by painting the walls light mocha, hanging wall sconces, building an Art Deco armoire, painting Deco patterns on the closet doors, installing lights around the bottom edge of the bed frame, hanging a canopy, and painting a faux-malachite finish on the furniture tops and wall sconces. Frank gets woodsy in a dining room, painting the walls deep orange, installing pine doors between the dining room and kitchen, creating a coffee table out of a large flowerpot, painting white birch trees all around the room, and making a large pig-topped weather vane to sit above the fireplace.

Notable: Edward makes his designer debut in this episode.

A Compliment?: Ty finishes installing the bed light, turns it on, and tells Edward, "It looks like Vegas!"

Getting Personal: Frank admits to a fear of heights.

Name Game: Frank names the weather vane pig "Poopalina."

Edward's Room: ☺ 😐 ☹
Frank's Room: ☺ 😐 ☹

Long Island: Split Rock Road ⑦

Cast: Paige, Genevieve, Vern, Amy Wynn

The Rooms: Gen brightens a dark kitchen by painting the walls white, the trim celadon green, the window shutters pale blue, and the cabinets yellow. Gen also polishes the existing copper stove hood, hangs white wooden slats on one wall, builds a butcher-block table, skirts the dining chairs in white fabric, and coats a new light fixture with copper spray paint. Vern adds a soft touch to a kitchen by painting the walls and cabinet door insets green, painting parts of the cabinet doors white, stenciling white fleurs-de-lis on the cabinet doors, building a new laminate countertop, laying a two-tone parquet floor, using green toile fabrics on Roman shades and table linens, adding touches of green gingham to the tablecloth, and adding several green-shaded table lamps to the countertop.

Dance Break: Gen dances to shake a can of spray paint.

What Was She Thinking?: Wanting to make candleholders out of pieces of rock, Gen tries to drill into the rock with a carbide bit that she was assured could handle the job. (Didn't she remember the California: Peralta Street episode in which Hildi had similar problems?!) After several attempts, Gen looks into the camera and says, "I suggest buying candleholders at the local hardware store."

Notable: Gen's inspiration for her design is a necklace that the homeowner wears nearly every day.

Gen's Room: ☺ 😐 ☹
Vern's Room: ☺ 😐 ☹

New York: Whitlock Road 👶

Cast: Paige, Genevieve, Doug, Amy Wynn

The Rooms: Gen designs a bedroom with an espresso color scheme: She paints the walls café au lait, uses darker java on the ceiling beams, and paints sections of the ceiling cream. She also sews orange asterisks on a white bedspread, builds a combination headboard/desk, and exposes original wood flooring. Doug updates a bedroom by painting squares on the wall in multiple shades of sage, building a mantel-like headboard, designing S-shape side tables, sewing stripes of yarn on a white bedspread, and framing strips of wood veneer for bedside art.

Fashion Report: Paige wears a tank top or, rather, several matching tank tops featuring phrases that relate to each scene of the show: Key Swap, Blue Team, Red Team, Gen, and Doug.

Yucky Moment: Gen and Amy Wynn shoot an air compressor hose into their mouths, blowing out their cheeks.

Faux Arrest: During the end credit shots, Paige is handcuffed by a local police officer.

Budget Boasting: Gen's total costs amount to $763 and some change—the lowest budget quoted on camera thus far in the series.

Gen's Room: ☺ ☺ ☹
Doug's Room: ☺ ☺ ☹

New York: Half Hollow Turn

Cast: Paige, Frank, Kia, Amy Wynn

The Rooms: Frank brings a living room up-to-date by painting the walls bamboo yellow, adding black accents on the walls and the furniture, using concrete stepping-stones to create side tables, converting a garden bench into a coffee table, and hanging a custom sculpture made from electrical and plumbing components. Kia gets funky in a basement rec room by painting the walls purple and light green, building a wall-length bench with purple velvet upholstery, hanging a swirly purple wallpaper border, installing halogen lights on a running cable, and creating green draperies.

Notable: This is theme queen Kia's first episode on the show.

Budget Crisis: Paige uses too much spray paint on Frank's concrete stepping-stone project, but Frank doesn't have the money to buy more paint.

Yum!: After the final Reveal, one of the homeowners presents a cake with the entire *Trading Spaces* cast airbrushed on the frosting.

Frank's Room: ☺ ☺ ☹
Kia's Room: ☺ ☺ ☹

Philadelphia: 22nd Street

Cast: Paige, Edward, Genevieve, Ty

The Rooms: Edward adds ethnic flair to a living room by painting the walls red, texturing the fireplace with black paint and tissue paper, hanging an existing rug on the wall, building a chaise lounge with finial feet, and installing an entertainment center made of shadow boxes. Gen heads to Cuba in a bedroom by covering the walls with textured white paint, adding a faux-plank finish to the doors, building a headboard enhanced with a blown-up image from a Cuban cigar box, designing lighted plastic bed tables, and creating picture frames out of cigar boxes.

Notable: Gen's inspiration for her room is the entire country of Cuba. She's never been.

Quotable Quote: Gen: "When you're working with a $1,000 budget, you've got to faux it up a bit."

Edward's Room: ☺ ☺ ☹
Gen's Room: ☺ ☺ ☹

Philadelphia: Gettysburg Lane

Cast: Paige, Frank, Vern, Ty

The Rooms: Frank updates a kitchen by painting the walls and cabinets several different colors, laying a stone-look vinyl tile, installing a new countertop, adding decorative elements to a half-wall to create a new serving bar, and mounting plates with wooden food cutouts across the soffit. Vern adds his version of cottage style to a living room by painting the walls yellow, installing white wainscoting,

building a 12-foot-wide shelving and storage unit, framing large copies of old family photos, making a "quilt" of images to hang above the storage unit, and adding touches of denim fabric throughout the room.

Fashion Report: Vern shows off his legs by wearing shorts.

Quotable Quote: Frank's male homeowner tries to get out of faux-finishing, suggesting that it's a job for a woman. Frank says, "All of a sudden I feel like I have to go out and buy a dress for the prom because I do this all the time."

Yawn: Vern gets virtually no sleep between Days 1 and 2 because he's trying to help finish the built-in storage unit.

Yucky Moments: Ty has a running gag of using wood glue as lotion, rubbing it into his hands, face, and neck.

Frank's Room: ☺ ☺ ☹
Vern's Room: ☺ ☺ ☹

Pennsylvania: Gorski Lane

Cast: Paige, Frank, Doug, Ty

The Rooms: Frank adds a celestial touch in a bedroom by painting the ceiling deep plum and painting silver stars across it. He paints the walls with several shades of cream and green, adds small blocks of color to the paneled doors, builds a writing desk, hangs a small cabinet upside down on the wall, and makes several pieces of custom artwork. Doug brings some "jungle boogie" to a bedroom by painting zebra stripes across all four walls, painting the ceiling dark brown, suspending a bamboo grid from the ceiling, and covering the existing headboard with sticks and bamboo.

Fashion Report: Doug shows off his legs by wearing shorts and flip-flops. There are also several buttons undone on his shirt.

Quotable Quote: When Frank unveils his purple paint, he says to his homeowners, "Prepare yourselves for the final squeal."

Oops!: While Ty is helping one of Frank's homeowners install a ceiling fan, Ty's drill falls from his ladder and lands on the fan, shattering the glass. (Ty eventually buys a new ceiling fan, paying for it himself so that it doesn't come out of Frank's budget.)

Conflict: One of Doug's homeowners is very concerned about covering the walls with zebra stripes. As she tries to talk him out of doing it, Doug says, "There's no way you're gonna stop me, so don't even try."

Resourceful: Doug wants to include a table but doesn't have extra money in his budget to pay for lumber. Ty ends up digging through the trash for scrap timber to make it.

Frank's Room: ☺ ☺ ☹
Doug's Room: ☺ ☺ ☹

Long Island: Dover Court

Cast: Paige, Vern, Edward, Amy Wynn

The Rooms: Vern sets a boy's bedroom in motion by painting the walls various shades of blue, building a race car bed with working headlights, suspending a working train track and toy planes from the ceiling, and hanging a motorcycle swing made from recycled tires. Edward brings the outdoors into a bedroom by painting the walls moss green and antiquing a landscape print. He alters prefab side tables with filigreelike cuts, disguises ugly lamps with black spray paint and fabric slipcovers, hangs antique glass shutters over the windows, and builds a large entertainment center, using the existing side tables and glass shutters.

Notable: Vern's homeowner keeps saying "sweet," and Vern tries to claim the word is his.

Resourceful: Having heard that Vern is doing a "planes, trains, and automobiles" room, neighborhood kids want to give him pictures of all three to hang in the room. Vern likes the idea but points out that he doesn't have the money to pay them. The kids donate the pictures, which Vern then incorporates into the room.

Confession Time: While sewing, Edward's male homeowner admits that his wife is better than he is with power tools.

Vern's Room: ☺ ☺ ☹
Edward's Room: ☺ ☺ ☹

Pennsylvania: Victoria Drive

Cast: Paige, Doug, Kia, Amy Wynn

The Rooms: Doug creates a cabin feel in a living room by covering the walls in brown Venetian plaster, hanging red Roman shades, covering a prefab coffee table with leather, staining the existing sofa and coffee tables, sewing cow-print pillows, building a large armoire covered with rough-cut poplar, and hanging leftover lumber on the walls in decorative stripes. Kia creates her version of an indoor garden in a guest bedroom by painting the walls yellow, hanging a flowery wallpaper border on the ceiling, creating a duvet out of synthetic turf and silk flowers, building a headboard from a tree limb, hanging a chair swing from a cedar arbor, placing gravel under the swing, and building a picket fence room divider.

Fashion Report: In keeping with the theme of her room, Kia wears overalls and a straw hat.

Yucky Moment: When Doug's homeowners enter the room to meet him at the start of the show, Doug is barefoot and enjoying a plate of brownies. Doug offers to share, but his team turns down the offer because Doug's feet are close to the plate. Doug then taps his foot across the top of the brownies and offers them again.

Quotable Quote: Doug defends his dark stain choice by saying, "I would not damage anything of quality. I only damage things that are crappy."

Impressive Impersonation: Kia does her best Gary Coleman by saying, "Wha'choo talkin' 'bout, Amy Wynn?"

Doug's Room: ☺ ☺ ☹
Kia's Room: ☺ ☺ ☹

New Jersey: Manitoba Trail

Cast: Paige, Frank, Doug, Amy Wynn

The Rooms: Frank goes all out in a country living/dining room by painting the walls light green, distressing the floors, painting a faux rug under the coffee table, applying several decorative paint colors and finishes to an antique cabinet, building custom lamps with large antique yarn spools, and creating three homemade country-girl dolls out of pillow forms. Doug brightens a living room by painting everything—the walls, ceiling, ceiling beams, fireplace, and ceiling fans—bright white ("White Whoa"). He buys two new white sofas, hangs bright blue draperies, installs a new doorbell that blends into the white wall, sews many brightly colored throw pillows, makes a large framed mirror, and creates custom art pieces.

Foot Fetish: Doug goes barefoot while painting a white border on a natural rug and puts his bare feet near his female homeowner's head while she sews pillows.

Reveal-ing Moment: The male living/dining room homeowner is so happy about his room that he kisses Paige.

Frank's Room: ☺ ☺ ☹
Doug's Room: ☺ ☺ ☹

Nazareth: First Street

Cast: Paige, Vern, Doug, Amy Wynn

The Rooms: Vern adds a touch of serenity to a living room by painting three walls taupe and one wall deep blue, adding a new mantel, sewing throw pillows with a wave motif, suspending mini symbiotic environments from the ceiling, building a coffee table with a center inset of sand and candles, and placing six fountains around the fireplace. Doug gives a kitchen an earthy feel by laying brown peel-and-stick vinyl flooring, painting the walls beige, making new orange laminate countertops, painting the cabinets yellow with an orange glaze, adding crown molding to the cabinet tops, building a pie safe, and upholstering the dining chairs with red-orange fabric.

Fashion Report: Vern's pants fall down as he's running during the opening segment.

Notable: Amy Wynn and Doug have a food fight during the end credits.

Vern's Room: ☺ 😐 ☹
Doug's Room: ☺ 😐 ☹

New Jersey: Catania Court ✳ $

Cast: Paige, Hildi, Genevieve, Amy Wynn

The Rooms: Hildi has the golden touch in a bedroom: She paints the walls yellow-green, sews bedding with fabrics she purchased in India, uses batik-inspired stamps to create gold accents on the ceiling and around the room, replaces the existing baseboards with taller ones, adds a gold wash to the existing furniture, builds a low-slung "opium couch," and hangs a vintage glass light fixture. Gen finds the silver lining in a dining room: She paints the walls carnelian red, hangs silver crown molding, paints the trim and chair rail ivory, hangs ivory and silver draperies, paints a canvas floorcloth to lay under the table, and hangs a new light fixture that has small tree limbs attached to it.

Fashion Report: Hildi's male homeowner starts the show wearing heels, noting that he's chosen "Hildi-approved footwear." Hildi paints his toenails with the room paint. When the homeowner starts to take off the shoes in order to paint, Hildi tells him to put them back on, pointing out that she never goes barefoot on the job.

Ringing Inspiration: Gen gets her design idea from a piece of her own jewelry, a ring that came from Afghanistan.

Hildi's Room: ☺ 😐 ☹
Gen's Room: ☺ 😐 ☹

Philadelphia: East Avenue ?

Cast: Paige, Hildi, Frank, Amy Wynn

The Rooms: Hildi gets graphic in a living room by painting three walls yellow, covering one wall with a large Lichtenstein-inspired portrait of herself, adding a glass-shelf bar area, building all new tables and chairs, sewing cushions with mod pink and orange fabric, and re-covering a thrift store couch with red fabric. Frank brightens a living room by painting the walls deep purple, painting the ceiling bright red, designing a coffee table unit with four bases that move apart and become extra seating, and creating wall art with rain gutter materials and round wooden cutouts.

Notable: All four homeowners are members of the Philadelphia Charge, a professional women's soccer team.

Resourceful: After applying one coat of purple paint on the wall, Frank realizes that the original burgundy paint is showing through in patches, creating an unexpected faux finish. He decides to keep it that way.

Quotable Quote: While hanging draperies, Frank dispenses his wisdom, saying, "A little fluffing is good."

Reveal-ing Moments: The homeowners are "weirded out" by the Hildi portrait in their living room.

Hildi's Room: ☺ 😐 ☹
Frank's Room: ☺ 😐 ☹

Virginia: Gentle Heights Court $ ☹ ♥

Cast: Paige, Hildi, Kia, Ty

The Rooms: Hildi roughs it in a boy's bedroom by painting the walls and ceiling midnight blue, hanging a moon-shape light fixture, placing glow-in-the-dark stars on the ceiling, hanging a solar system mobile, building a 13-foot rock climbing wall, adding fold-up camping furniture, placing the mattress in a room-size tent, using a blue sleeping bag as a duvet, and placing camping lanterns around the room. Kia adds sensuous details to a bedroom by painting the walls orange, painting the trim Grecian blue, hanging a red and gold wallpaper border, creating a Taj Mahal cutout to place around the existing entertainment center, installing two

wooden columns from India, adding bedding made from sari fabrics, and suspending the bed from the ceiling with chains.

Guy Stuff: Ty (wearing a bike helmet for safety, of course) tries out the completed rock wall, falling to the floor.

Quotable Quote: When Kia asks Ty when he's going to hang the chains for her bed, he says, "Just as soon as you're through yanking mine."

Notable: A shirtless Ty suns himself during the end credits.

Reveal-ing Moments: Upon seeing the suspended bed in her newly decorated room, the female homeowner exclaims, "I wanna jump in there and get naked!"

Hildi's Room: ☺ 😐 ☹
Kia's Room: ☺ 😐 ☹

Arlington: First Road 💣 ✳ 👶 ?

Cast: Paige, Hildi, Doug, Ty

The Rooms: Hildi gift-wraps a bedroom by painting the walls "Tiffany box" aqua blue, adding a duvet and Roman shades in the same aqua blue, airbrushing white "ribbons" on the walls and fabrics, hanging white lamps with square shades above the headboard, building acrylic side tables that light up from inside, and adding bright silver accents. Doug warms up a bedroom by painting the walls and ceiling a deep gray-blue, hanging white Roman shades with brown silk curtains and cornice boards, constructing a headboard from a large existing window frame, balancing the headboard with a new armoire that features white silk door insets, and creating custom artwork in brown and navy.

Homework Blunder: For homework, Hildi has her team airbrush the "ribbons" on the walls. When she returns on Day 2, the project is complete but not quite the way she would have done it. (The "ribbons" are very large and look more like Keith Haring-inspired graffiti.)

Notable: One of Hildi's homeowners leaves an apology note on the wall in black marker. It says, "Hildi made me do it."

Conflict: Doug's homeowners fight him on every decision, including removing the ceiling fan, selecting paint colors, painting the ceiling, staining the floor, and accessorizing the room. Near the end of Day I, Doug washes his hands of the room and uses the PaigeCam to record instructions for making draperies. Paige then takes the camera to the homeowners and helps them make the curtains.

Quotable Quote: At a heated point in the conflict with his homeowners, Doug exclaims, "I can't continue to educate people on what's good taste!"

Reconciliation?: While Doug is reclining in a lawn chair reading a newspaper, his homeowners come to say that they need him after all. By the end of Day 2, Doug's female homeowner admits that the design is growing on her. Doug says, "It's growing on her like a fungus, but it's growing."

Hildi's Room: ☺ 😐 ☹
Doug's Room: ☺ 😐 ☹

Washington, D.C.: Quebec Place ✳

Cast: Paige, Genevieve, Vern, Ty

The Rooms: Gen dishes up a serene living room inspired by her favorite Thai soup. She paints the walls a light bone color and gives the room lemongrass green accents, a newly constructed sofa, a wall-length valance with lemongrass curtains, and lotus flower light fixtures. Vern turns up the heat in a newlywed couple's bedroom by painting the fireplace and dressing room red, installing a floor-to-ceiling mirrored wall in the dressing area, hanging rows of crystals above the fireplace, sewing red silk Roman blinds, and installing a large headboard with red silk insets.

Fashion Report: High heels abound in this episode: Both female homeowners wear them during the Key Swap and the Reveal; Gen wears them when first meeting the homeowners. Comfort and practicality win out, and everyone

quickly removes the shoes.

Notable: This episode is the first time Kia's and Edward's faces appear among the quick shots of the designers during the opening credits.

Oops!: When Ty attempts to install a wall-length valance he built for Gen's room, he discovers that he built it I foot too long. Much discussion ensues, and Ty eventually cuts 6 inches from each end.

Well, Thanks: Gen liberally hands out kudos, telling Ty that the couch he built is her favorite piece of furniture he's created during the series. She also tells her homeowners that their stain job on the sofa frame is the best anyone has done on the show.

Head Games: Vern's headboard is so large and unwieldy that he has to have a police car stop traffic so that he and his homeowner can carry it across the street. After they get it inside, they find it's too large to go up a flight of stairs, and Ty has to cut length off the bottom to fix the situation.

Resourceful: Vern initially planned to restore the hardwood floor in his room, but by the end of Day 2, he shows Paige the large red rug he has purchased to hide the floor, which is not shaping up as he had hoped.

Reveal-ing Moments: The male homeowner on one of the teams is so happy, he kisses Paige on both cheeks. His wife likes the makeover so much, she says she doesn't even care that he's kissing another woman.

Gen's Room: ☺ 😐 ☹
Vern's Room: ☺ 😐 ☹

Indiana: River Valley Drive

Cast: Paige, Doug, Genevieve, Amy Wynn

The Rooms: Gen tones down an overly bright living room by painting the walls a sleek silver-gray, painting existing furniture white, designing a new entertainment center made out of stacked white boxes with punched-aluminum door insets, and adding a few bold touches of color with green curtains, a new green room screen, and a fuchsia ottoman. Doug puts his foot down in his "Back from Brazil" living room, hanging a three-section painting of his own foot. He also stencils white flowers—inspired by sarongs—on the walls, slipcovers the existing furniture in white, extends the fireplace mantel, designs an acrylic plastic light fixture, and sews throw pillows out of tie-dyed sarongs.

Ouch!: During B-roll footage, Gen bounces a basketball off her head as if it were a soccer ball. Doug looks concerned and kisses her forehead.

Musical Moment: Gen plays guitar for Amy Wynn during the end credits, making up a song about kicking Amy Wynn's butt if she doesn't finish her carpentry projects. She's a little off-key.

Huh?: Doug's original stencil idea takes too long, and he has to design another one that he thinks will be easier. It isn't. During the Reveal, the homeowners seem confused by the stenciling and ask, "What is that? An olive?"

Gen's Room: ☺ 😐 ☹
Doug's Room: ☺ 😐 ☹

Indiana: Fieldhurst Lane ✳ ☹ 🔌

Cast: Paige, Doug, Vern, Amy Wynn

The Rooms: Doug gets back to his Midwestern roots in a bedroom by painting the walls orange, installing padded tan wainscoting, creating custom paintings of wheat and corn, embellishing simple white bedding with orange ribbon and yarn, and designing a large armoire. Vern sets a restful scene in a bedroom by painting the walls a light blue, attaching oak plywood squares to a wall, painting the existing furniture black, reupholstering a chaise longue with dark blue velvet, hanging blue velvet draperies, wrapping the bed frame with white beaded garland, and installing new sconces and a ceiling fixture with white beaded shades.

Farm Fun: During the opening, Doug drives a tractor, Paige milks a cow, and Vern and Amy Wynn put up hay bales.

Name Game: Doug gets a little confused about the name of his room, calling it at various times "Sunset Harvest," "Harvest Sunset," "Indian Sunset," and "Golden Harvest"— all of which are Doug-speak for orange.

Joke Time: At the start of Day 2, Doug tells his homeowners that he doesn't like the bright orange walls and that they're going to have to repaint them light green. Paige tells Doug no, Doug insists, and they storm off arguing. Doug reenters with brushes and starts painting a wall himself. When the homeowners finally relent and pick up brushes, Doug laughs and says, "Gotcha!" His female homeowner gets the last laugh though, slapping Doug's face with her green paint-covered brush.

Hair Care: During the end credits, Paige points out Vern's emerging bald spot.

Kiss-Off: When Paige says goodbye at the end of the show, all four homeowners blow a kiss toward the camera à la *The Dating Game.*

Doug's Room: ☺ 😐 ☹
Vern's Room: ☺ 😐 ☹

Indiana: Halleck Way $ 👶 ❓ 🔌

Cast: Paige, Edward, Kia, Amy Wynn

The Rooms: Edward designs a soft yet masculine bedroom by painting the tray ceiling slate blue and white, painting the walls and existing furniture tan, hanging a customized light fixture with a hand-painted glass frame, draping white fabric across the length of one wall, hanging lush brown draperies, and slipcovering the head- and footboards. He also rearranges the furniture and creates neoclassic wall shelves. Kia walks like an Egyptian in a bedroom by painting the walls "Tut Wine" and "Pharaoh Gold," building pyramid-shape cornice boards, and hanging framed Egyptian prints and a handmade Eye of Horace. She also paints a personalized hieroglyphic message for the homeowners ("David loves Noel") on an existing room screen and installs a ceiling fan with palm leaves attached to the blades.

Vroom: Edward and Kia drive a race car at the Indianapolis Motor Speedway.

Quotable Quote: Toward the end of Day 2, Edward tells Paige that the room is "kind of coming together." Paige responds by saying, "Yeah, if you stress the words 'kind of.'"

Diva Fit!: Early in Day I, Kia's homeowners run out of paint during the first coat. Kia blames the homeowners' painting ability; Paige blames Kia's paint calculations. Kia eventually gives the homeowners a painting lesson in an attempt to salvage what paint she has left. They wind up having to buy another gallon.

Scare Flair: During a bumper shot, Paige enters wrapped up in toilet paper like a mummy.

Ouch!: When Kia discovers her male homeowner and Amy Wynn installing cornice boards without installing the curtain rods first, she takes a piece of fabric, wraps it around the homeowner's neck, and pretends to strangle him.

Fountain Follies: Kia spends much of her budget on a pyramid-shape fountain that she designed herself. The fountain is the subject of many discussions, including questions about its construction, sealant, and pump mechanism (Amy Wynn works on this while squatting in the homeowners' water-filled bathtub). Late on Day 2, Kia and her team meet up with Amy Wynn and an obviously leaky

fountain; they decide to chuck the whole thing at the last minute.

Edward's Room: ☺ 😐 ☹
Kia's Room: ☺ 😐 ☹

Missouri: Sunburst Drive ✳

Cast: Paige, Genevieve, Vern, Ty

The Rooms: Gen draws inspiration for a bedroom from gauchos, Argentine cowboys: She paints the walls deep brown, creates faux crown molding, installs a woven leather-and-red-velvet headboard, and glues pictures of gauchos to the closet doors. She also builds an upholstered bench and pulls in furniture from other rooms. Vern adds a masculine edge to a girlie bedroom by painting the walls soft blue, painting the existing furniture and doors red, designing a wall-length desk and computer hutch, installing a headboard made of upholstered leather squares, and adding several Moroccan wrought-iron light fixtures and accents.

Fashion Report: The cast members wear monogrammed bowling shirts and bowl during the B-roll footage. Gen bowls barefoot.

Quotable Quote: When Gen's female homeowner mentions that she's nervous about her own room, Gen reassures her by saying, "Do you like clean lines and straight things? Vern does."

Silly Gen!: Paige chastises Gen and her team for falling behind on Day I, asking them what they've gotten done. Gen sheepishly replies, "We've laughed a lot."

More Gen: While working with her female homeowner to upholster a bench, Gen shows her how to use cardboard to keep a straight, professional-looking line when finishing off the edges. She then says jokingly under her breath, "Because that's all we are on this show—a bunch of professionals."

Gen's Room: ☺ 😐 ☹
Vern's Room: ☺ 😐 ☹

Scott Air Force Base: Ash Creek ❓ 😖

Cast: Paige, Doug, Kia, Ty

The Rooms: Doug travels down Route 66 in a child's bedroom by laying gray carpet, painting highway stripes and road signs on the walls, and installing a front and back end from two actual cars. (He adds a mattress in the back end of one car, and the front end of the other car serves as a toy chest.) Kia creates "Military Chic" in a living/dining room, using various shades of gray paint, new chair rails, a gray and white camouflage wallpaper border, pillows and cushions in the same camouflage, a new storage bench, a faux fireplace, a red slipcover, red accents, and draperies made from a gray parachute.

Take It Easy: During Load Out, Doug sits in a child's chair as his homeowners do all the work. They eventually carry the chair out of the room—with Doug in it.

Family Ties: As Doug reveals his design idea to Ty, a Wilson Trucking semi drives up loaded with the two car halves. It then becomes an act from a circus, as seven people start filing out of the cab. Doug introduces them as his brothers, nephews, and friends—all of whom are there to help carry the car halves around.

Car-nival: Getting the cars into the room is insanely difficult and time-consuming. The front end doesn't fit down the hallway and has to be sawed in half and reassembled inside the room. Ty spends so much time on Doug's cars that he has to cut one of Kia's projects.

Drop In: Kia meets her homeowners after having supposedly parachuted onto the roof.

Shocking Confession: Kia admits to her female homeowner that she's "never used a slipcover before."

Fashion Report: During Designer Chat, Kia wears an outfit that seems to consist of several layers of multicolor printed fabrics. It boggles the mind.

Doug's Room: ☺ 😐 ☹
Kia's Room: ☺ 😐 ☹

Missouri: Sweetbriar Lane ⊣🔳 ❓

Cast: Paige, Edward, Frank, Ty

The Rooms: Edward designs a sleek bedroom by painting the walls shades of gray, white, and China blue, adding extra closet and storage space, and designing a mirrored entertainment armoire to hide the TV. He also hangs a light fixture wrapped in pearls, adds gray, purple, blue, and green fabrics, and creates a sculpture out of curled metal. Frank creates an unusual bedroom, painting the walls orange and installing large eyes made of copper tubing above the bed. An upholstered lip headboard completes the face, and a new platform bed stands beneath it. Frank paints the fireplace purple and creates an artistic theme by installing a giant pencil on one wall and painting sketches of women around it.

Edward's Design Theory: "I always think you need a touch of black in a room."

Heavy Metal: Gushing about his metal sculpture during Designer Chat, Edward tells Paige that he wants to make more pieces like it because he enjoyed the sparks flying when he sawed into the metal.

Ouch?: During the Carpenter Consult, Frank jokingly knocks Ty to the ground. Ty milks the experience by wearing a neck brace for the rest of the show and acting as though he's in constant pain anytime he's near Frank.

Southern Belle: When Paige jokes about the layered tulle "petticoat" lampshades that Frank has designed, Frank smugly admits, "During the Civil War, I used to make 'em for the troops."

Quotable Quote: Frank tells Paige that he used her lips as inspiration for his headboard. She's impressed that he noticed her lips, and he replies, "I may be old, but I'm not dead."

Frank the Vampire Slayer? During the end credits, an extended shot of Frank shows him carving the giant pencil out of a piece of unpainted wood. Frank tells the camera that he's making a vampire stake and cautions viewers to be careful who they stake, because "anyone walking around after dawn is not a vampire."

Edward's Room: ☺ 😐 ☹
Frank's Room: ☺ 😐 ☹

London: Garden Flat 🔌 $

Cast: Paige, Genevieve, Hildi, Handy Andy of *Changing Rooms*

The Rooms: Gen enlivens a bedroom by painting the walls a rich, spicy orange, painting a small alcove red, and hanging many yellow-green draperies. She builds a new platform bed with drawers underneath, adds a prefab dresser, and creates an unusual closet space along one wall. She also installs crown molding and hangs rows of framed Chinese newsprint. Hildi brightens a girls' bedroom by splattering bright paint on white walls, laying fluffy white carpet, framing the girls' artwork, and sewing rainbow-color draperies. She also installs doors on an existing wall-size shelving unit, builds beds and nightstands on casters, and creates a "secret garden" area with wheat grass plants.

Notable: This is the first "International Challenge" between *Trading Spaces* and its sister show, *Changing Rooms.*

Dialect Differences: Paige mangles a British accent repeatedly and, not surprisingly, has major trouble understanding Handy Andy. Later, Gen tries to explain the concept of crown molding to Handy Andy, who eventually explains that the British call the same thing "coving."

Weather Woes: Gale-force winds upset the show on Day 2, blowing the Carpentry World tent into a neighboring yard. Gen, Paige, and Handy Andy jump over the neighbor's fence and try to put the tent back into place. After getting it back in the right spot, but not getting it to stand up completely, Handy Andy turns to the two giggling women and dismisses them, saying, "You've annoyed me enough now."

More Weather Woes: While struggling with the tent, Handy Andy points out that the old slate tiles on nearby roofs may blow off and hit people below. This seriously upsets Paige, who decides to move the prefab dresser assembly project inside.

Messy Madam: After throwing paint on the walls, Hildi is completely covered in paint (a *Trading Spaces* first?). She apparently didn't remember her own advice to a paint-covered Dez in Lawrenceville: Pine Lane (Season I): "Delegate, delegate, delegate!"

Yucky Moment: When Hildi asks whether she's gotten all the paint off her face, Paige gleefully informs her that a spot of yellow paint in the middle of Hildi's nose resembles a "whitehead zit." Hildi is grossed out.

Hildi's Room: ☺ 😐 ☹
Gen's Room: ☺ 😐 ☹

Mississippi: Golden Pond ✳

Cast: Paige, Laurie, Hildi, Amy Wynn

The Rooms: Laurie updates a bedroom by painting the walls camel-yellow, building a large headboard of upholstered aqua fabric with a chocolate brown grid overlay, creating a large mirror from smaller mirrored squares, hanging a thrift store chandelier, adding newly upholstered thrift store chairs, using aqua and camel-yellow bedding, and building new chocolate brown bookcases. Hildi adds color to a bathroom (a *Trading Spaces* first!) by stapling more than 6,000 silk flowers to the walls, painting the trim and cabinets gold, creating red acrylic cabinet door insets, building a bench upholstered in terry cloth, and sewing draperies and a shower curtain out of floral fabrics from France.

Notable: This is Laurie's first episode back after maternity leave. Baby Gibson makes a quick appearance on the morning of Day 2.

Tub Time: While sitting (apparently naked) in a tub full of bubbles, the bathroom homeowners describe what they'd like to see done to their room.

Ouch!: Laurie's male homeowner injured his foot by driving his motorcycle into a building. He tells Paige that it was a learning experience, much like *Trading Spaces*, adding that *Trading Spaces* is "slightly more interesting and almost as painful" as hitting that wall.

For Laughs: Laurie is in high spirits this episode, hula-hooping during a bumper shot, doing a bad approximation of a New Jersey accent during the end credits, and doing her best impression of an upholstered headboard for her homeowners.

Hildi's Room: ☺ 😐 ☹
Laurie's Room: ☺ 😐 ☹

Mississippi: Winsmere Way ✳ 🔌

Cast: Paige, Laurie, Hildi, Amy Wynn

The Rooms: Laurie spices up the bedroom of a newly divorced homeowner with cumin yellow walls, an eggplant ceiling, a large upholstered headboard with nailhead trim, a new chaise lounge, a blown-glass light fixture, and two upholstered message boards. Hildi adds drama to a bedroom by covering the walls in red toile fabric, painting the ceiling smoky plum, slipcovering a thrift store sofa with cream fabric, building a new armoire with curved doors, repainting two thrift store lamps, and creating shadow boxes.

Deco-Dramas: Laurie has some traumatic moments during the episode. Her purple ceiling isn't quite the eggplant shade she had hoped for (she calls it "Disco '70s Nightmare" and goes out to find new paint). Later, Laurie doesn't have enough ribbon to create her message boards. Her homeowners save the day by designing a new pattern for the ribbon. Laurie gushes that she's so glad when she has smart homeowners.

More Deco-Dramas: Laurie's "smart homeowners" have moments of their own though: While hanging two towel bars that act as magazine racks, they nearly destroy the wall trying to put in wall anchors and can't seem to get the racks level. During the end credits there is a shot of them working on this project, and the male homeowner says, "They don't show the real-life crap."

Lounge Act: Laurie states that the chaise is the best piece Amy Wynn has ever built for her and points out that "every Southern woman needs a chaise longue."

Oops!: While attaching the toile fabric to the walls, Hildi accidentally shoots a staple at Paige's rear end. It doesn't go in, but Paige notices it.

Hildi's Design Theory: "I can see the beauty in many things."

Under Where? When she begins to glaze a dresser, Hildi opens the drawers to find that they hadn't been emptied. The top drawer is full of underwear, which Hildi grabs by the handful and throws at her homeowners. One homeowner exclaims, "It's raining panties!"

Hildi's Room: ☺ 😐 ☹
Laurie's Room: ☺ 😐 ☹

San Antonio: Ghostbridge ✳ ☹

Cast: Paige, Hildi, Vern, Ty

The Rooms: Hildi gets groovy in a living room by lining one wall with record albums and painting the remaining walls purple, yellow, teal, and orange. She creates slipcovers in the same colors, makes a coffee table top by covering a colorful scarf with a large piece of glass, paints the homeowners' favorite chair black with brightly colored flowers, installs lamps made from French drainpipes, and designs a large entertainment center. Vern leaves his mark in a living room by covering one wall with wood veneer wallpaper, bringing in new pieces of brown furniture, hanging red draperies, creating a red and gold leaf coffee table and room screen, and laying a red rug.

Notable: Hildi refers to herself as "the Slipcover Queen."

Happy Feet: When Ty and Hildi's male homeowner bring in the base for the entertainment center, Hildi jumps on it and starts dancing before they've had a chance to put it down.

Dream Team?: Vern refers to his homeowners and himself as the "Obsessive-Compulsive Disorder Triplets." His homeowners agree.

Attraction Action: One of Vern's homeowners has a serious crush on Vern and Ty. During the episode, she hits on both Ty and Vern, protects Vern from criticism, and refers to Vern as "my Vern."

Reveal-ing Moment: The album room homeowner isn't sure about her room and keeps repeating, "This is...unique."

Hildi's Room: ☺ 😐 ☹
Vern's Room: ☺ 😐 ☹

Austin: Wyoming Valley Drive

Cast: Paige, Laurie, Hildi, Ty

The Rooms: Laurie adds warmth to a dining room by weaving one wall with brown sueded cotton and painting the other walls pink-orange. She builds a round dining table with a stenciled top and a fabric skirt, designs a buffet table with legs made from plumbing conduit, and makes draperies and seat cushions out of green fabric. Hildi creates a sleek kitchen by covering the walls with peel-and-stick wine labels, painting the cabinets black, deepening an existing bench, designing a large pot rack out of lumber and copper plumbing conduit, painting the existing wooden blinds black and orange, slipcovering the dining chairs with orange fabric, and embellishing the dining table with gold accents.

Quotable Quote: Paige asks the dining room homeowners what they're afraid of finding when they return home. The female homeowner says that she doesn't want any type of neon color, and Paige replies sarcastically, "Yeah, because Laurie is known for neon."

Design Differences: An ongoing debate about whether the kitchen homeowners will like having more than 4,000 wine labels stuck to their walls consumes much of the episode. Their neighbors continually point out that the homeowners don't drink or keep any type of alcohol in their home. Hildi adjusts her vision a bit, converting her design for a wine rack into a pot rack, but the wine labels stay.

Hildi's Design Theory: "I try to show people different things to do with the obvious."

Reveal-ing Moment: The kitchen homeowners aren't thrilled with the labels. Their neighbors enter the room at the end of the show with a steamer, tied with a ribbon, that can be used to remove the labels.

Hildi's Room: ☺ 😐 ☹
Laurie's Room: ☺ 😐 ☹

Austin: Aire Libre Drive $ 🔌 ☹

Cast: Paige, Frank, Kia, Ty

The Rooms: Frank adds drama to a living room by painting one wall orange and the other walls yellow, building two new end tables, designing a massive coffee table out of a black granite slab and four decorative columns, adding a toy chest to hold the homeowners' dog toys, covering the existing furniture with multicolor fabric, and laying a new rug. Kia updates a living room by painting the walls moss and brown, painting a golden glaze on the brown wall, designing new draperies out of various types of printed fabric, building a large frame above the fireplace, adding a new love seat, and scavenging accessories from other rooms in the house.

Fashion Report: The cowboy hat officially becomes the most common *Trading Spaces* fashion accessory, with Paige donning one in the Opener.

Budget Crisis: Frank is already $123 over budget when his homeowners meet him on Day I. He manages to return enough things over the course of the show that he's under budget by Designer Chat.

Yucky Moment: While trying to hang Kia's mirror, Ty accidentally breaks the wire on the back of the frame. As Paige is trying to decide what to do, Ty pretends to floss Paige's teeth with the broken wire. (He evidently didn't hear Doug's warning about this practice in Philadelphia: Valley Road.)

Lazy Days: Because Kia and Frank's combined carpentry load takes only a few minutes to complete, Ty decides to organize and clean the *Trading Spaces* trailer and enlists the help of neighborhood kids. One of Kia's homeowners wants to work with Ty even though Ty

171

doesn't have anything to do, so Ty pretends to teach him to use a broom. During Day 2, Frank finds Ty relaxing in a hot tub. Paige feels so sorry for Ty, she lets him call Time's Up.

Mad Dash: Kia summarizes her design philosophy for the room as "redecorating by relocating." During the Hurry-Up sequence, Kia and her homeowners run around the house finding items to accessorize the room. Kia and her female homeowner find several items, but the male homeowner returns with only an unattractive Mardi Gras-theme egg.

Last Laughs: During the end credits, Paige rides Ty like a horse; Ty demonstrates his pole-vaulting ability with a piece of Kia's lumber, breaking the board in midair.

Frank's Room: ☺ 😐 ☹
Kia's Room: ☺ 😐 ☹

Austin: Wampton Way ●᠅✳

Cast: Paige, Genevieve, Doug, Ty

The Rooms: Gen adds an Art Deco touch to a living room by color-washing the walls in various shades of yellow and orange, slipcovering the existing furniture with graphic black and white fabric, building up the existing fireplace with black and mahogany accents, suspending the television with cables and a wooden shelf, adding two large topiaries, and framing various champagne and liqueur posters. Doug gives a living room an antique Spanish flair by building a large dark brown fireplace facade, painting the walls smoky green, and staining existing barstools darker brown. He adds a chair upholstered in newspaper-print fabric and creates wall art with canvas and newspapers.

Sideshow: Theatrical weirdness abounds during the Opener: Gen, Doug, and Ty wear costumes and bad wigs while performing a magic trick (Doug cuts Ty in half with a chain saw while Gen strikes poses). Paige makes herself disappear.

Attraction Action?: When entering the room for the first time, Gen's male homeowner (who works as a stand-up comedian) says to Ty, "Man, Ty, you *are* hot!"

Name Game: For no apparent reason, Doug's male homeowner calls him "Sparky."

Quotable Quote: Gen's female homeowner has never made a slipcover but admits that she made three Jedi Halloween costumes for her kids. Gen's reply: "Jedi costumes equal slipcovers to me."

Musical Moment: Doug plays trombone in a bumper shot.

Surprise!: During Load Out, Gen's team removes the existing sectional couch and finds a body outline underneath, planted as a joke by the homeowners.

Yucky Moment #1: Gen's male homeowner, who's been known to streak, goes outside to work with Ty wearing nothing but a tool belt and strategically placed paint chips. Noting that Ty is flustered, the homeowner suggests coming back later, turns to walk away, and exposes his rear to the camera.

More Yucky Moments: Gen's homeowners suggest that instead of buying rags, they could use their neighbors' underwear to apply the color wash to the walls. Later, PaigeCam footage shows Gen digging through the male homeowner's underwear drawer. Gen presents the selected boxers to her team and proceeds to wear a pair on her head. Her team follows suit.

Show Time: Gen tests the strength of the suspended entertainment shelf by dancing on it. Ty and Gen's male homeowner give her dollar bills.

Waterworks?: Paige asks Doug whether redoing the fireplace will upset the homeowners (referring to Seattle: 137th Street in Season 2). Doug assures Paige that these homeowners will "only cry tears of joy."

Fashion Report: During Designer Chat Gen wears the same dress as the woman in one of the champagne posters used for design inspiration.

Doug's Design Theory: "Every room has to have a little quirk in it."

Gen's Room: ☺ 😐 ☹
Doug's Room: ☺ 😐 ☹

San Diego: Camino Mojado ☹ ✳

Cast: Paige, Vern, Genevieve, Ty

The Rooms: Gen adds Polynesian flair to a bedroom by building a grass-cloth headboard, hanging mosquito netting, painting the walls smoky taupe, painting the existing furniture orange, sewing two new dog beds out of the same material as the new bedspread, planting several large palm plants, and building a large square shelving unit to hold accessories and a TV. Vern cozies up a loft TV room by attaching several upholstered diamond shapes on two walls, building new black velvet sofas, designing a large black coffee table with upholstered panels, framing photocopies of Hollywood movie legends on vellum, installing new shelving to hold entertainment equipment, and hanging several black and taupe drapery panels to close off the room.

Notable: Gen admits that she's allergic to dogs.

Oops!: Gen's grass-cloth headboard completely falls apart when Ty and Gen's female homeowner try to move it off a construction table.

Farm Fetish?: When Gen's homeowners tell her that they're not really worried about what Vern may be doing to their home, Gen jokes that Vern has been wanting to explore new design avenues, including "the barnyard look." Oddly enough, the next scene shows Vern telling his female homeowner to stuff a pillow as she would stuff a turkey.

Cabinet Chaos: Ty changes Gen's cabinet design, adding several time-consuming decorative elements. The piece isn't finished by the morning of Day 2, and Gen asks Ty to finish building the piece and add the decorative elements later if he has time. Later, Paige finds Ty doing decorative work on the uncompleted piece; she reads him the riot act. Ty eventually finishes the piece at the last minute, only to find that it's too big to be easily carried up the stairs.

Vern's Room: ☺ 😐 ☹
Gen's Room: ☺ 😐 ☹

San Diego: Dusty Trail

Cast: Paige, Doug, Genevieve, Ty

The Rooms: Doug designs a bedroom he calls "Cosmo Shab" by color-washing the walls with three shades of blue paint, painting the cathedral ceiling gray, installing crown molding, hanging a chandelier from the dining room, sewing gray and white toile draperies, painting the existing furniture white, and distressing the newly painted pieces to create an antique look. Gen transforms a kitchen into a French *boucherie* (butcher shop) by covering the walls with green chalkboard paint, painting the cabinets vanilla with gray insets, installing a tin ceiling, building a larger tabletop, and hanging pictures of "meat puppets" around the room.

Fashion Report: The cast members wear wet suits, and Ty successfully surfs during B-roll footage.

Mini Diva Fit: Paige tells Doug's female homeowner, "You have perfect teeth." Doug is put out that Paige doesn't say the same about him.

New Toy: Doug and Ty have fun with a new piece of equipment—a laser-pointer level that is the size of a large tape measure.

Baby Boom: As she hands a respirator mask to her pregnant female homeowner, Gen says, "This paint is a little bit toxic, and I want your baby to be born with all its fingers and toes." She then cites Ty as an example of what could happen to the woman's child if she doesn't wear a mask.

Kudos: Gen says of Doug, "He might have a lot of attitude, but he's a damn fine designer."

Tardy Tin: The tin for Gen's ceiling doesn't arrive until the morning of Day 2, after getting stuck somewhere in Nebraska. Because Ty has to work on Doug's house, Gen's male homeowner installs the tin himself. For the Reveal, most of the tin is installed, with the exception of a small strip at the edge of the room. Gen informs viewers, "Tin is not a two-day project, just so you know."

French Flair: Gen wears a beret during Designer Chat and says, "Ooh la la, my room rocks!"

Quotable Quote: When the female bedroom homeowner sees her room, she says, "I feel so bad for saying all that bad stuff about Doug!"

Gen's Room: ☺ 😐 ☹
Doug's Room: ☺ 😐 ☹

San Diego: Fairfield ❓ 😮 🔌 ☹

Cast: Paige, Kia, Frank, Ty

The Rooms: Kia updates an office/game room by painting the walls apricot and the trim orange. She builds a strange love seat that sits 8 inches off the ground, designs a removable tabletop for an existing game table, builds storage cubes that double as seats, hangs a "mirror" made of CDs, makes chess pieces out of copper pipe, and rearranges the existing desk to create a more effective office area. Frank fluffs a "tranquil love nest" in a bedroom, adding coffee-color paint, a new coffee bar (complete with a small refrigerator), wooden chevrons on the existing furniture, gauzy fabric draped around the four-poster bed, and a large piece of bamboo for a drapery rod.

Oops!: Frank's male homeowner bought new shoes for the show but steps in a full paint tray early in Day 1.

Blind Ambition: Kia's window treatment plan is a fiasco: The blinds must be dismantled, hand-numbered (there are more than 150 of them), covered with spray adhesive, and attached to a piece of fabric. Each slat is then supposed to be cut apart and restrung so that either the fabric side or copper side is exposed. Midway through Day 2, Kia's male homeowner has only completed 1½ blinds, and the finished product looks horrible; he tells Paige, "If I were in charge, she [Kia] wouldn't get away with this." Paige tries to convince Kia to consider alternatives. Kia states that "there's no other plan!" In the end, the room doesn't have any window coverings.

Wise Words: Frank encourages his male homeowner while they're stuffing pillows by saying, "Become one with your batting."

Mirror Image: Paige asks whether Kia expects the homeowners to be able to see themselves in the CD "mirror" Kia designed. Kia and Paige debate the reflectiveness of the CDs until Kia finally looks at herself in a CD and says, "I'm a little distorted and very prismed, but I can see myself clearly." Paige doesn't buy it but helps with the project anyway.

Quotable Quote: During Designer Chat Frank tells Paige, "Romance doesn't have to be, like, socko-wow leather and lace."

Frank's Room: ☺ 😐 ☹
Kia's Room: ☺ 😐 ☹

San Diego: Duenda Road

Cast: Paige, Frank, Vern, Amy Wynn

The Rooms: Frank adds romance to a bedroom by painting the walls soft green, building a canopy frame out of molding strips, hanging a gauzy canopy from the ceiling, and revamping an existing dresser. Vern updates a living room by painting the walls with two tones of soft green, surrounding the existing fireplace with slate tiles, painting the existing furniture a third shade of green, hanging glass vases on the wall, installing green chenille draperies, and creating a new entertainment center.

Aquatic Antics: Most of the B-roll footage for the episode is the cast hanging out at SeaWorld. Frank kisses a dolphin, Paige talks to killer whales, Vern rides a dolphin, and Amy Wynn has all sorts of adorable escapades with a seal and a sea otter.

Quotable Frank: Frank-isms abound in this episode. Some highlights: "You don't have to strangle the roller, Mary. The roller is your friend, Mary." When a homeowner says that Frank's body is in the way of something the homeowner needs to see, Frank retorts, "My body's in the way of the entire wall!" Frank also accidentally calls his female homeowner "babe," only to realize the slip (and apologize for it) a few moments later.

Confession Time: Amy Wynn confides to the camera, "It's so hard getting used to all these different people's houses; you have no idea!"

International Flair: When Frank tells Paige that something is merely a suggestion, she replies, "Oh, kind of like a stoplight in Italy?"

Girl Time: Amy Wynn gushes about the function of the furniture piece she's building by saying, "Oh my God, shoe storage! I love it!"

Double Duty: Vern and his male homeowner joke that the wall vases can hold flowers or be beer dispensers.

Wise Words: During Designer Chat, Paige tells Vern, "You can't spend money to buy time."

Notable: Check out the end credits to see Paige and Frank demonstrate the "nonstop action" of *Trading Spaces*.

Frank's Room: ☺ 😐 ☹
Vern's Room: ☺ 😐 ☹

Los Angeles: Murrietta Avenue ⓢ

Cast: Paige, Genevieve, Laurie, Amy Wynn

The Rooms: Gen gives a bland living/dining room a 1940s L.A. twist by painting the walls dark red, painting the trim bright white, adding white crown molding, and hanging draperies featuring a palm frond print. Gen also designs lighted display shelves, frames book illustrations of 1940s L.A., reupholsters the dining room chairs with more palm frond fabrics, and hangs a new period light fixture. Laurie creates a warm and comfortable living room by painting the walls butter yellow, with bands of golden camel and cream near the top of the walls. She installs built-in wall cabinets to house electronic equipment and "hideaway dog beds," lays a large khaki area rug, paints the fireplace white, slipcovers the sofa, and adds two green chenille chairs.

Ouch!: During the Opener, Gen and Amy Wynn watch as a tattoo artist inks the *Trading Spaces* logo onto Laurie's bicep.

Yucky Moment: As Gen cleans off a cluttered entertainment center shelf, she encounters the cremated remains of two dogs, stored in boxes with little dog statues on top of them. She's a little ooked out.

Girl Fight?: Gen jokingly contrasts her design style with Laurie's, claiming Laurie always manages to delegate tasks.

Gen then assumes a Southern accent and says, "Y'all, it's time to paint." Yet somehow, Gen still gets stuck doing the painting.

Musical Moment: Paige dances and spray-paints dining chairs while Gen's male homeowner plays polka music on the accordion.

Musical Moment, Part 2: Gen's male homeowner is a semicelebrity. He plays guitar and has toured with Alice Cooper, Slash, Guns N' Roses, and Carole King. (One of these things is not like the other...)

Musical Moment, Part 3: Slash (who's good friends with Gen's homeowner and a *Trading Spaces* fan) hangs out with Gen and the homeowner in Sewing World. Gen tells Slash to sit down and learn to sew too. He does.

Southern Charm: Laurie finds out on Day 2 that the carpet she ordered won't arrive for two more days. She and Paige go shopping and find a carpet Laurie likes. When Laurie asks the very nice carpet salesman (who happens to be friends with Gen's male homeowner, whose room Laurie is redoing) if the carpet is in her price range (she can only spend $45), he does some quick calculations with a calculator and says, "We're gonna make it in your price range." Laurie hugs him.

Notable: The end credits feature a long shot of *everyone* (and we mean everyone) doing a kick line.

Gen's Room: ☺ 😐 ☹
Laurie's Room: ☺ 😐 ☹

Las Vegas: Carlsbad Caverns 💣✳

Cast: Paige, Hildi, Doug, Amy Wynn

The Rooms: To redecorate a living room, Hildi draws inspiration from a print she bought in London. She paints the walls dark red, paints the ceiling blue with light purple glaze, adds six red columns throughout the room, lays checkerboard vinyl flooring in two shades of orange, hangs deep red draperies, and adds slipcovers, upholstery, and pillows in every shade of the rainbow. Doug gets "Dirty" in a bedroom by covering the walls in dark brown Venetian plaster; he paints the ceiling peach, hangs bright blue draperies, sews pillows and bedding in various blue fabrics, installs crown molding, builds a large round white armoire, and creates a four-poster look around the existing bed with four alleged stripper poles.

Happy Couple?: During the Opener, Hildi and Doug go to a drive-through wedding chapel where Amy Wynn officiates. After Amy Wynn ominously says, "You are wed," Hildi and Doug kiss. Hildi pulls away and says, "Stop opening your mouth!" Doug looks coyly into the camera and shrugs his shoulders.

Thread-Bare: On the morning of Day 2, Hildi discovers that the fabric she shipped isn't going to arrive in time. She goes speed-shopping for fabric and must frantically sew everything in one afternoon.

Take That!: When Doug's male homeowner complains about painting the ceiling peach, Doug harasses him by asking what color the carpet is in his house. The carpet is a disgusting pink, so Doug tells the homeowner that because of his crappy carpet color he doesn't get a say in color choices.

Navel Alert!: No, not Paige. This time it's Amy Wynn showing her navel—for a long time while installing Doug's stripper poles.

Notable: The Reveals for this episode originally aired live.

Fame Game: Vegas celebs aplenty in this episode! Using a drill, Penn & Teller perform a card trick for Amy Wynn; Robin Leach presents Doug and his team with champagne and compliments them on upping the style in their homes;

Rita Rudner does the splits; and an Elvis impersonator helps Doug hang valances while singing "Amazing Paint." Only in Vegas, baby, only in Vegas.

Hildi's Room: ☺ 😐 ☹
Doug's Room: ☺ 😐 ☹

173

General Index : Trading Spaces Make It Yours!

Use the following index as your handy guide to locating the topics, tools, looks, styles, and designers you're looking for. Jump in!

A-B

Acrylic
 cabinet panels, 151
 cutting, 156
 nightstands, 127
 shelving, 52
Anchors, 54
Armoire, 29, 59, 63, 113, 119
Artwork
 abstract, 112
 CDs, 145
 Eye of Horus, 99
 newspaper decoupage, 121
 photographs, 51, 95
 posters, 19
 solar system, 139
 vases, 80
Bargain shopping, 34-35, 65, 79, 128
Beads
 crystals, 40, 57
 lampshade, 45, 47
 pillows, 45
 seed, 7

Beds
 four-poster, 63
 hanging, 148
 inflatable, 141
 platform, 13
Bench, upholstered, 155
Buttons, 17, 116, 121

C-E

Cabinets
 acrylic panels, 151
 creative ideas, 157
 painting tips, 155
 replacing panels, 156
Cable, 21, 22, 23
Candles
 sconces, 14, 21, 39, 119, 128, 155
 tea lights, 7
 votives, 57, 79
Canopy, tent, 139
Ceilings
 creative ideas, 109
 tin, 105
 tray, 112

vaulted, 13
Chalk line, 108
Chess set, 146
Child's room, 139-141
Classic style, 27-29, 33-35, 39-40
Combing, 41, 42
Cornices, 99, 100, 121
Countertop repair, 133
Cubes
 building basics, 148
 creative ideas, 149
 seating, 145
 shelving, 52
Curtains. *See* Window treatments
Customizing ideas, 7, 17, 31, 47, 77, 131
Decoupage, 77, 96, 121
Designers
 Doug, 39-40, 63-64, 119-121
 Edward, 33-35
 Frank, 45, 85-87
 Gen, 19-21, 51-52, 93-95, 105-106

Hildi, 27-29, 127-128, 139-141, 151-155
 Kia, 99, 145-146
 Laurie, 71-74, 111-115, 133
 Vern, 13-15, 57-59, 78-81
Display
 cabinets, 157
 collection, 52, 53
 multiples, 15, 57
 plates, 72
Distressed furniture, 123
Divider wall, 33, 37
Drills, cordless, 54
Elegant style, 19-21, 33-35, 127-128

F-H

Fabric
 application on walls, 27, 30
 bark cloth, 52-53
 on ceilings, 109
 divider wall, 37
 headboard, 116
 lampshade, 47
 velvet, 45, 93
 wall panels, 33
Fans, ceiling, 19, 99, 142
Faux
 finishes, 29, 39-43, 85, 87
 painting tools, 41-42
Feathers, 28, 41, 77
Fireplace
 fix-ups, 61
 mantel, 85
 painted, 57, 133
 slate, 79
 surround, 19, 119, 122
Flower walls, 151-155

Project Index — Find the perfect decorating project fast and easy.

A-F

Bolsters, 60
Cabinet panel replacement, 156
Cable, steel, 22
Ceiling fan replacement, 142
Ceramic tiles, 82
Chalkboard paint, 108
Cornice, 100
Cube, 148
Decoupage, 96
Fabric-covered walls, 30

Faux painting, 42
Fireplace surround, 122

H-R

Hanging heavy objects, 54
Headboard, upholstered, 116
Lamps/shades, customized, 47
Measuring, 134
Mirrors, customized, 77
Miters, cutting, 66
Pillows, customized, 17

Plywood, cutting, 16
Roman shades, 130

S-W

Screens, 88
Slipcovers, 36
Stamps/stencils, 46
Tables, customized, 131
Tin ceilings, 107
Weaving, 76

Furniture
  custom-made, 31, 131
  multifunctional, 145
  painted, 40
  restoration guidelines, 60
Glaze, 39–40, 42
Glue gun, 28, 116, 152
Glues, 7, 17, 28, 96
Hammers, 75
Headboards
  creative ideas, 117
  fabric, 57, 111
  leather, 93
  moldings, 67
  slip covered, 33
  upholstered, 116
Hook-and-loop tape, 71

I–N

Inspirational ideas, 93, 139, 151
International themes
  East Indian, 45
  Egyptian, 99
  French, 27–29, 105–106
  Madrid, 71–73
  Mediterranean, 85–87
  South American, 93–95
Lamps/shades, 47
Leather, 64, 71, 77, 93
Level, 15, 79, 86
Lighting fixtures
  acrylic nightstands, 127
  ceiling light, 13, 28, 115
  chandelier, 34, 40, 73
  creative ideas, 139, 141, 143, 151
  downlights, 57
  pendant, 57
  puck, 33
  replacing ceiling fan, 142
  swing-arm, 80
Linens, 13, 40, 45, 58, 63, 127, 139
Longue chair, 111
Magazine racks, 115
Measuring basics, 134
Medallions, 19, 34
Media center, 14, 21, 23, 81

Message board, 113
Mirrors
  bathroom, 154
  customized, 77
  sconces, 15
  tiles, 58
Miter box, 66
Moldings
  ceiling medallions, 19, 34
  creative ideas, 39, 67
  crown, 51, 63, 64, 152–153
  cutting miters, 66
  fireplace, 119, 122
  plywood edges, 14
Multipurpose room, 145–146
Nail gun, 13, 116
Nail head trim, 76, 111, 115, 133

O–R

Opaque projector, 95, 127
Ottomans, 135
Painting techniques
  block of color, 23, 80
  cabinets, 155
  chalkboard, 105, 106, 108
  clear polyurethane sealer, 13, 14
  distressed, 123
  faux finishes, 29, 39–43, 61, 85, 87
  glaze, 39–40, 42
  leather look, 64
  linen look, 42
  pens/markers, 7, 34, 130
  spray, 129
  stamping, 41, 46, 101, 130
  stenciling, 45, 46, 71, 101, 127, 130
  using deep colors, 51
Pens/markers, paint, 7, 34, 130
Photographs, 95, 97
Pillows
  appliqué, 60
  bark cloth, 53
  bolster, 33, 60, 93
  customized, 17, 31
Plywood, 14, 16, 141

Quiz, attitude, 8–9
Ribbon, 114, 130
Rock-climbing wall, 141
Roman shades, 59, 128, 130
Room arranging, 35, 37
Router, 153

S–W

Safety tips
  saws, 16, 100
  spray painting, 129
Sander, electric, 147
Saws
  blades, 16, 59, 100, 156
  circular, 66, 100
  jigsaw/saber, 59, 66
  safety tips, 16, 100
  table, 16, 156
  tile, 82
Screens, 88–89, 99
Sewing machine, 95
Shadow boxes, 27
Shelving
  creative ideas, 23, 55
  display, 52, 72, 85
  plywood, 14
  for TV, 20, 21
Slipcovers
  couch, 20, 27, 79, 133
  headboard, 33
  making, 36
  ottoman, 135
  padding, 35
  wood, 146
Square, 86
Stamping, 41, 46, 101, 127
Staple guns, 116, 151
Stenciling, 45, 46, 71, 101, 127, 130
Storage
  chests, 57
  creative ideas, 157
  media center, 23, 81, 133
  wood cubes, 145
Stud finder, 140
Table skirt, 71
Tables, 74, 85, 87, 131, 145, 146
Themes, 74, 139, 151. See also

International themes
Tile nippers, 82
Tiles
  basics, 81
  creative ideas, 61, 83
  installing, 82
  mirror, 58
  slate, 79
  terra-cotta, 71
  tools, 82
Tin ceilings, 105, 107
Voltage tester, 142
Warm styles, 13–15, 93
Weaving, 76, 93
Window treatments
  bark cloth, 52, 53
  cafe curtains, 152
  cardboard rods/finials, 35
  clip-on curtains, 22, 73
  cornices, 99, 100, 121
  creative ideas, 101
  faux window, 34
  Roman shades, 59, 128, 130
  room darkening, 87
  stenciled, 45
Wire cutters, 22
Wood
  maple sheets, 13
  medium-density fiberboard, 14
  plywood, 14, 16, 141